NEW YORK CITY

1767.

NEW YORK

HISTORIC TOWNS.

Edited by Edward A. Freeman, D.C.L., and Rev. William Hunt.

NEW YORK.

BY

THEODORE ROOSEVELT,

Author of " The Winning of the West," etc.

With Three Maps.   Crown 8vo, 250 pages.

London and New York : LONGMANS, GREEN, & CO.

NEW YORK

THEODORE ROOSEVELT

Abridged and Illustrated

LEVENGER
PRESS

Delray Beach, Florida

Published by Levenger Press
420 South Congress Avenue
Delray Beach, Florida 33445 USA
800.544.0880
www.Levengerpress.com

This edition is an abridgment of the 1891 edition published by
Longmans, Green, and Co.
The endpaper map is from this earlier edition.

All illustrations, including the cover image, are used with permission
from the Picture Collection, The Branch Libraries, The New York
Public Library, Astor, Lenox and Tilden Foundations.

Library of Congress Cataloging-in-Publication Data

Roosevelt, Theodore, 1858-1919.
  New York / Theodore Roosevelt.
      p. cm.
"Abridged and illustrated."
  ISBN 1-929154-15-1 (Hardcover)
  1. New York (N.Y.)–History. I. Title.
F128.3.R79 2004
974.7'1–dc22

                                2003024515

Cover and book design by Levenger Studios
Mim Harrison, Editor
Printed in Singapore

Contents

Publisher's Preface   vii

1609-1647
Discovery and First Settlement
The Dutch Town Under the First Three Directors   1

1647-1664
Stuyvesant and the End of Dutch Rule   27

1664-1674
New Amsterdam Becomes New York
The Beginning of English Rule   37

1674-1720
New York Under the Stuarts
The Growth of the Colonial Seaport   49

1720-1764
The Close of the Colonial Period   63

1764-1774
The Unrest Before the Revolution   81

1775-1783
The Revolutionary War   91

CONTENTS

1783-1800
The Federalist City   121

1801-1821
The Beginning of Democratic Rule   139

1821-1860
The Growth of the Commercial and Democratic City   153

1860-1890
Recent History   169

Acknowledgments   187

Publisher's Preface

It may seem ironic that the man famous for being a Rough Rider and a western rancher wrote a history of that most urban of locales, New York City. But Theodore Roosevelt was first and last a New Yorker.

He was born at 28 East 20th Street, near Gramercy Park, on October 27, 1858. He grew up on West 57th, and early in his marriage to Alice, took up residence at a brownstone at 55 West 45th. His first political office was as a New York State Assemblyman in 1881, and he ran (unsuccessfully) for mayor of New York City in 1886.

Then in 1895, Theodore Roosevelt became a member of the New York City Police Commission and one of the city's most ardent reformers. From his Knickerbocker father, TR had soaked up his high moral sense of civic-mindedness, and he set to raiding the city's brothels and ridding New York of some of its deadliest tenements.

PUBLISHER'S PREFACE

The Metropolitan Museum of Art, the American Museum of Natural History and the Bronx Zoo all have the stamp of Roosevelt on them.

For all his love of rugged outdoor adventure, Roosevelt was also a serious reader and a prolific writer who had eight books under his belt by his early thirties. He was a man of action and a man of ideas.

That sounds like a New Yorker to me.

For my wife, Lori, and me, New York has always had a special place in our hearts. It is where we met. And when we founded our company in 1987, it was New Yorkers who first responded to our advertisements for reading lights. So we were delighted to discover this little-known history of the city by one of our country's best-known figures.

One of the best ways to get to know a city is to see it with someone who was born and raised there. We present to you Old New York, through the eyes of one of its sons.

– Steve Leveen

First hotel of New Amsterdam, 1642.

1609-1647
Discovery and First Settlement. The Dutch Town Under the First Three Directors.

THE HISTORY of New York deserves to be studied for more than one reason. It is the history of the largest English-speaking city which the English conquered but did not found, and in which though the English law and governmental system have ever been supreme, yet the bulk of the population, composed as it is and ever has been of many shifting strains, has never been English. Again, for the past hundred years, it is the history of a wonderfully prosperous trading-city, the largest in the world in which the democratic plan has ever been faithfully tried for so long a time; and the trial, made under some exceptional advantages and some equally exceptional disadvantages, is of immense interest, alike for the measure in which it has succeeded and for the measure in which it has failed.

In 1621, the great West India Company was chartered by the States-general, and given the monopoly of the American trade; and it was by this company that the city was really founded, the first settlement being made which was intended to be permanent. All the magnificent territory discovered by Hudson was granted it under the name of the New Netherlands. The company was one of

> *The paths of commerce were no less dangerous than those of war.*

the three or four huge commercial corporations of imperial power that played no small part in shaping the world's destiny during the two centuries immediately preceding the present. It was in its constitution and history archetypical of the time. The great trading-city of America was really founded by no one individual, nor yet by any national government, but by a great trading corporation, created however to fight and to bear rule no less than to carry on commerce. The merchants who formed the West India Company were granted the right to exercise powers such as belong to sovereign States, because the task to which they set themselves was one of such incredible magnitude and danger that it could be done only on such terms. They were soldiers and sailors no less than traders; it was only merchants of iron will and restless daring who could reap the golden harvests in those perilous sea-fields, where all save the strongest surely perished. The paths of commerce were no less dangerous than those of war.

The West India Company was formed for trade, and for peopling the world's waste spaces: and it was also formed to carry on fierce war against the public enemy, the King of Spain. It made war or peace as best suited it; it gave governors and judges to colonies and to conquered lands; it founded cities, and built forts; and it hired mighty admirals to lead to battle and plunder, the ships of its many fleets. Some of the most successful and heroic feats of arms in the history of the Netherlands were performed by the sailors in the pay of this company; steel in their hands brought greater profit than gold;

and the fortunate stockholders of Amsterdam and Zealand received enormous dividends from the sale of the spoil of the sacked cities of Brazil, and of the captured treasure-ships which had once formed part of the Spanish "silver fleet."

In the midst of this turmoil of fighting and trading, the company had little time to think of colonizing. Nevertheless, in 1624 some families of protestant Walloons were sent to the Hudson in the ship "New Netherland," a few of them staying on Manhattan Island. The following summer several more families arrived, and the city may be said to have been really founded, the dwellers on Manhattan Island after that date including permanent settlers besides the mere transient fur-traders. Finally in May, 1626, the director Peter Minuit, a Westphalian, appointed by the company as first governor of the colony, arrived in the harbour in his ship the "Sea-Mew," leading a band of true colonists,—men who brought with them their wives and little ones, their cattle and their household goods, and who settled down in the land with the purpose of holding it for themselves and for their children's children.

NEW YORK

With the arrival of Director Minuit, the settlement at the mouth of the Hudson first took on permanent form and became an organized community. He bought Manhattan Island from its Indian owners for the sum of sixty guilders, or about twenty-four dollars, and during the summer founded thereon a little town, christened New Amsterdam. It soon grew to contain some two hundred souls. Even at the beginning, the population was composed of peoples diverse in race and speech; not only were there Dutchmen and Walloons, but also even thus early a few Huguenots, Germans, and Englishmen.

The island was then a mass of tangled, frowning forest, fringed with melancholy marshes, which near the present site of Canal Street approached so close together from either side that they almost made another small island of the southern end. The settlers staked out a fort on the southernmost point, and huddled near it in their squalid huts; while they closely watched their cattle, which were in imminent

Even at the beginning, the population was composed of peoples diverse in race and speech.

danger from wolves, bears, and panthers whenever they strayed into the woodland.

Minuit was a kindly man, of firm temper, much energy, and considerable executive capacity; on the whole he was by far the best of the four directors who successively ruled the city and colony during the forty years of the Dutch supremacy. But the scheme of colonization was defective in more than one vital particular. The settlement was undertaken primarily in the interest of a great commercial corporation, and only secondarily in the interests of the settlers themselves. The world had not yet grasped the fact that those who went abroad to build mighty States in far-off lands ought by rights to be themselves the main beneficiaries of their toil and peril. A colony was considered as being established chiefly for the good of the colonists. The West India Company wished well to its settlers, who were granted complete religious freedom, and in practice a very considerable amount of civil liberty likewise; but after all, the company held that the first duty of the New Netherlands colony was to return large dividends to the company's stockholders, and especially to advance the worldly welfare of the company's most influential directors. It sought to establish a chain of trading-posts which should bring great wealth to the mother country, rather than to lay the foundations of a transatlantic nation of Dutch freemen. Hence, the settlers never felt a very fervent loyalty for the government under which they lived, and in its moment of mortal peril betrayed small inclination to risk their lives and property in a quarrel which was hardly their own.

This attitude of the old West India Company was that naturally adopted by all such corporations. It was curiously paralleled, even in our own day, by the way in which the great Hudson Bay Company shut the fertile valleys of the Red River and the Saskatchawan to all settlement. It was a thoroughly unhealthy attitude.

Minuit was active in establishing friendly relations with the savages. His boats explored the neighbouring creeks and inlets, and the Indians were well treated whenever they came to the little hamlet on Manhattan Island. In consequence they freely brought their stores of valuable furs for barter and sale. For two or three years the trade proved profitable, while, from other causes, the stock of the company rose to a high premium on the exchanges of Holland.

In 1628, for the purpose of promoting immigration, an act was passed granting to any man who should bring over a colony of fifty souls a large tract of land and various privileges, with the title of "Patroon." These patroons were really great feudal lords, who farmed out their vast estates to tenants who held the ground on various conditions. Their domains were often as large as old-world principalities; as an instance, Rensselaerswyck, the property of the Patroon Van Rensselaer, was a tract containing a thousand square miles. The introduction of this very aristocratic system was another evidence of the unwisdom of the governing powers. Moreover, the patroons, whose extensive privileges were curtailed in certain directions,—notably in that they were forbidden to enter into the lucrative fur-trade, the chief source of profit to the company,—soon began to rebel against these restrictions.

They quarreled fiercely with the company's representatives, and traded on their own account with the Indians; and the various private traders not only cut into the company's profits, but also, being amenable to no law, soon greatly demoralized the savages.

The settlers on Manhattan Island were not treated as freemen, but as the vassals of the company. For many years they were not even given any title to the land on which they built their houses, being considered simply as tenants at will. Minuit, it is true, chose from among them an Advisory Council, but it could literally only advise, and in the last resort the company had absolute power. The citizens had certain officers of their own, but they were powerless in the event of any struggle with the director. When the latter was, like Minuit, a sensible, well-disposed man, affairs went well enough, and the people were allowed to govern themselves, and were happy; but a director of tyrannous temper always had it in his power to rule the colony almost as if he were an absolute despot.

For six years Minuit remained in New Amsterdam, ruling the people mildly, preserving by a mixture of tact and firmness friendly relations with the Indians and with his English neighbours to the eastward,—to whom he sent a special embassy, which was most courteously received,—and keeping on good terms with the powerful and haughty patroons. During these years the trade of the colony increased and flourished, rich cargoes of valuable furs being sent to Holland in the homeward-bound ships, and the population of Manhattan Island gradually grew in numbers and wealth. Farms or "boueries" were established; and the settlers raised wheat, rye, buckwheat, flax, and beans, while their herds and flocks throve apace. The company soon built a mill, a brewery, a bakery, and great warehouses, and society began to gain some of the more essential comforts of civilization. Nevertheless, the company quarreled with Minuit. He was accused of unduly favouring the patroons, whose private ventures in the fur-trade were encroaching upon the company's profits, and moreover he had been drawn into a scheme of ship-building, which though successful,—a very large and fine ship being built and launched in the bay,—nevertheless proved much too expensive for the taste of his employers. Accordingly, he was recalled; and later on, deeming himself to have been ill-treated, he took service under the Swedish queen.

His successor was Wouter Van Twiller, who reached New Amsterdam early in 1633. Van Twiller was a good-natured, corpulent, wine-bibbing Dutchman, loose of life, and not over-strict in principle, and with a slow, irresolute mind. However, as he was an easy-going man his rule did not bear hardly on the colonists, while he won for himself an honourable reputation by devoting much of his time to the construction of public buildings. Thus, he made a new fort of earthen banks with stone bastions, enclosing within its walls not only the soldiers' barracks, but also at first the governmental residence and public offices; he also built several windmills and the first church which was used solely as such, as well as houses for the dominie and for the *scout-fiscal*. The latter was the most important of the local officers; he possessed curious and extensive powers, being the chief executive of the local government, and answering roughly to both the English sheriff and town constable, though with a far wider and more complicated range of duties. The colony had at this time received two important additions in the shape of the first school-master—who failed ingloriously in his vocation, and then tried to eke out his scanty salary by taking in *washing*,—and the first regular clergyman. The clergyman, Dominie Bogardus, was a man of mark and of high character, though his hot temper made him unpopular.

Both England and Holland claimed the country, each wishing it really more for purposes of trade than of colonization.

Van Twiller kept on fairly friendly terms with the Indians, though causes of quarrel between the settlers and the savages were constantly arising. Plenty of wrong was done on each side, and it would be hard to say where the original ground of offence lay. Probably the whites could not have avoided a war in the end; but they certainly by their recklessness and brutality did all in their power to provoke the already suspicious and treacherous red men. The history of the dealings of the Dutch with the Indians is not pleasant reading.

Under Van Twiller there were endless troubles with the English. Both England and Holland claimed the country from the Connecticut to the Delaware, each wishing it really more for purposes of trade than of colonization; and the quarrels generally arose over efforts of rival vessels of the two nationalities to control the trade with some special band of savages. In Van Twiller's time an English vessel entered the Hudson and sailed to the head of navigation, where she anchored and began to barter with the savages for their furs; whereupon the Dutch soldiers from the neighbouring fort fell upon her and drove her off, confiscating the furs. At the same time Van Twiller built a fort and established a garrison on the Connecticut, threatening to hold it by force against the English; but when the pinch came the Hollanders failed to make their threats good, and the Puritans from Plymouth sailed up the river and took possession of the banks in defiance of their foes.

Better luck attended Van Twiller's efforts on the Delaware, the Cavaliers proving easier to deal with than the Roundheads. The Dutch had already built a colony on this river; but the colonists became embroiled with the Indians, who fell on them and massacred them to a man. Then a party of Virginians established themselves in one of the deserted Dutch forts, and set about founding a settlement and trading-post; but when the news was brought to the director at New Amsterdam, he promptly despatched a party of troops against the invaders, who were all taken captive and brought in triumph to Manhattan Island. Van Twiller hardly knew what to do with them; so he scolded them soundly for the enormity of their offence in trespassing on Dutch territory, and then shipped them back to Virginia again.

The internal affairs of the colony went more smoothly. There were occasional quarrels with the powerful patroons, but the director was much too fond of his ease, and of wine and high living to oppress or rule harshly the commonalty; and the value of the trade with the home country on the whole increased, though it never became sufficient to make the company take very much thought for its new possession. But Van Twiller though easy going to the people was not an honest or faithful servant to the company in matters financial; and in 1637 he was removed from his office on the charge of having diverted the moneys of the corporation to his own private use.

His successor, Wilhelm Kieft, was much the worst of the four Dutch governors. Unlike his predecessor, he was industrious and temperate; but he possessed no talent whatever for managing men, and had the mean, cruel temper of a petty despot. His mercantile reputation was also none of the best; though during his administration he himself kept reasonably clear of financial scandals. In fact, the West India Company was

The Hollanders were traders and seafarers, and they found it hard to settle down into farmers, who alone can make permanent colonists.

tired of a colony which proved a drain on its revenue rather than a source of profit; and any second-rate man, who bade fair not to trouble the people at home, was deemed good enough to be governor of such an unpromising spot.

Kieft found the New Netherlands in a far from flourishing condition. The Dutch colonists, though stubborn and resolute, were somewhat sluggish and heavy tempered, without the restless energy of their far more numerous and ever-encroaching neighbours on the east (the New Englanders), and lacking the intense desire for what was almost mere adventure, which drove the French hither and thither through the far-off wilderness. Population had increased but slowly, and the town which huddled round the fort on the south point of Manhattan Island was still little more than a collection of poor hovels. The Hollanders were traders and seafarers, and they found it hard to settle down into farmers, who alone can make permanent colonists. Moreover, at the outset they were naturally unable to adapt themselves to the special and peculiar needs of their condition. The frontier and frontier life date back to the days when the first little struggling settlements were dotted down on the Atlantic seaboard, as islets in a waste of savagery; but it always took at least a generation effectively to transform a European colonist into an American frontiersman. Thus the early Dutch settlers took slowly and with reluctance to that all-important tool and weapon of the American pioneer, the axe, and chopped down very little timber indeed. As a consequence, they lived in dugouts or cabins of bark and poles, lacking the knowledge to build the log huts, which always formed the first and characteristic dwellings of the true backwoodsmen. It was a good many years before the backwoods type, so characteristically American, had opportunity to develop.

Kieft was not well pleased with the colony, and the colony was still less pleased with Kieft. From the beginning he took the tone of a tyrant, treating the colonists as his subjects. He appointed as council but one man, a Huguenot of good repute, named La Montagne, and then, to prevent all danger of a tie, decreed that La Montagne should have but one vote and he himself two. He then filled the different local offices with his own flatterers and sycophants, and proceeded to govern by a series of edicts, which were posted on the trees, barns, and fences; some of them, such as those forbidding the sale of fire-arms and gunpowder to the Indians, were good; while great discontent was excited by others, such as the sumptuary laws (for he made a bold attempt to stop the drinking and carousing of the mirth-loving settlers), the establishing of a passport system, and the interference with private affairs by settling when people should go to bed, labourers go to work, and the like. The Dutch were essentially free and liberty loving, and accustomed to considerable self-government; and the Manhattan colonists felt that they were unjustly discriminated against, and chafed under the petty tyranny to which they were exposed.

However, under Kieft the appearance of the town was much improved. Streets began to be laid out, and a better class of private houses sprang up, while a new church and the first tavern—a great clumsy inn, the property of the company—

were built, and the farms made good progress, fruit-trees being planted and fine cattle imported. New settlements were made on the banks of the Hudson and the Sound, on Staten Island, and on what is now the Jersey shore. The company made great efforts further to encourage immigration, allowing many privileges to the poorer class of immigrants, and continuing, in diminishing form, some of the exceptional advantages granted to the rich men who should form small colonies. The colonists received the right to manufacture, hitherto denied them; but, unfortunately, the hereditary privileges of the patroons were continued, including their right of feudal jurisdiction, and the

There was almost complete religious toleration, and hence many Baptists and Quakers took refuge, fleeing from the persecutions of the Puritans.

exclusive right to hunt, fish, fowl, and grind corn on their vast estates. The leader in pushing these new settlements, and one of the most attractive figures in our early colonial history, was the Patroon de Vries, a handsome, gallant, adventurous man, of brave and generous nature. He was greatly beloved by the Indians, to whom he was always both firm and kind; and the settlers likewise loved and respected him, for he never trespassed on their rights, and was their leader in every work of danger, whether in exploring strange coasts or in fronting human foes.

Besides the Dutch immigrants, many others of different nationalities came in, particularly English from the New England colonies; and all, upon taking the oath of allegiance, were treated exactly alike. There was almost complete religious toleration, and hence many Baptists and Quakers took refuge among the Hollanders, fleeing from the persecutions of the Puritans.

All this time there was continual squabbling with the neighbouring and rival settlements of European powers. A large body of Swedes, under Minuit, arrived at and claimed the ownership of the mouth of the Delaware, bidding defiance to the threats the Dutch made that they would oust them; while the English, in spite of many protests, took final possession of the Connecticut valley and the eastern half of Long Island. But the distinguishing feature of Kieft's administration was the succession of bloody Indian struggles waged between 1640 and 1645.

For these wars Kieft himself was mainly responsible, though the settlers and savages were already irritated with each other. Occasional murders and outrages were committed by each side. The Indians became alarmed at the increase in numbers of the whites, and the whites became tired of having a horde of lazy, filthy, cruel beggars always crowding into their houses, killing their cattle, and by their very presence threatening their families. A strong and discreet man might have preserved peace; but Kieft was rash, cruel, and irresolute, and precipitated the contest by ordering a brutal vengeance to be taken on the Raritan tribe for a wrong which they probably had not committed. They of course retaliated in kind, and there followed a series of struggles, separated by short periods of patched-up truce. Kieft took care to keep shut up in the fort, away from all possible harm, whereat the settlers murmured greatly. All their wisest and best men, including the Patroon de Vries, the councilman La Montagne, and Dominie Bogardus, protested against his course in bringing on the war.

Early in 1643, he caused by his orders, one of the most horrible massacres by which our annals have ever been disgraced. The dreaded Mohawks had made a sudden foray on the River Indians, who, like the other neighbouring tribes, were Algonquins; and the latter, fleeing in terror from their adversaries, took refuge close to the wooden walls of New Amsterdam, where they were at first kindly received. On Shrovetide night, Kieft, with a hideous and almost inconceivable barbarity and treachery, as short-sighted as it was cowardly, caused bodies of troops to fall on two parties of these helpless and unsuspecting fugitives, and butchered over a hundred.

This inhuman outrage at once roused every Indian to take a terrible vengeance, and to wipe out his wrongs in fire and blood. All the tribes fell on the Dutch at once, and in a short time destroyed every outlying farm and all the smaller settlements, bringing ruin and desolation upon the entire province, while the surviving settlers gathered in New Amsterdam and in a few of the best fortified smaller villages. The Indians put their prisoners to death with dreadful tortures, and in at least one instance the Dutch retaliated in kind. Neither side spared the women and children. The hemmed-in Dutch sent bands of their soldiers, assisted by parties of New England mercenaries, under a famous woodland fighter, Capt. John Underhill, against the Indian towns. They were enabled to strike crippling blows at their enemies, because the latter foolishly clung to their stockaded villages, where the whites could surround them, keep them from breaking out by means of their superiority in firearms, and then set the wooden huts aflame and mercilessly destroy, with torch or bullet, all the inmates, sometimes to the number of several hundred souls. These Indian stockades offered the best means of defence against rival savages; but they were no protection against the whites, who, on the other hand, were much inferior to the red men in battle in the open forest.

At first the Indians did not understand this; and in their ignorance they persisted in fighting their new foes in the very

This popular meeting may be considered as the first fore-shadowing of our whole present system of popular government.

way that gave the latter most advantage. It was in consequence of this that the seventeenth-century Algonquins suffered not a few slaughtering defeats at the hands of the New Englanders and New Netherlanders.

Finally, crippled and exhausted, both sides were glad to make peace; and the whites again spread out to their ruined farms. In his dire need Kieft had summoned a popular meeting and chosen from among the heads of families a council of twelve men to advise him in the war. This popular meeting was the first of its kind ever held on Manhattan, and may be considered as the first fore-shadowing of our whole present system of popular government. The Council of Twelve at once proceeded to protest against the director's arbitrary powers, and to demand increased rights for the people, and a larger measure of self-government. Instantly Kieft dissolved them; but later on, when the settlement seemed at the last gasp, a council of eight was chosen, this time by popular vote, and took advantage of the dread of the public enemy to demand the needed internal reforms. They protested in every way against Kieft's tyranny. The latter would not yield. The mutinous spirit became very strong; disorder, and even murder took place, and affairs began to drift toward anarchy. Numerous petitions were sent to Holland asking Kieft's removal, and finally this was granted. The harassed colony was given a new director in the shape of a gallant soldier named Peter Stuyvesant, who arrived and took possession of his office in May, 1647.

Peter Stuyvesant's town house, 1658.

1647-1664
Stuyvesant and the End of Dutch Rule.

GRIM OLD Stuyvesant had lost a leg in the wars. He wore
in its place a wooden one, laced with silver bands,—so that
some traditions speak of it as silver. No other figure of Dutch,
nor indeed of colonial days, is so well remembered; none other
has left so deep an impress on Manhattan history and tradition
as this whimsical and obstinate, but brave and gallant old fellow,
the kindly tyrant of the little colony. To this day he stands in a
certain sense as the typical father of the city. There are not a few
old New Yorkers who half-humorously pretend still to believe
the story which their forefathers handed down from generation
to generation,—the story that the ghost of Peter Stuyvesant, the
queer, kindly, self-willed old dictator, still haunts the city he
bullied and loved and sought to guard, and at night stumps to
and fro, with a shadowy wooden leg, through the aisles of

St. Mark's church, near the spot where his bones lie buried.

Stuyvesant was a man of strong character, whose personality impressed all with whom he came in contact. In many ways he stood as a good representative of his class,—the well-born commercial aristocracy of Holland. In his own person he illustrated, only with marked and individual emphasis, the strong and the weak sides of the rich traders, who knew how to fight and rule, who feared God and loved liberty, who held their heads high and sought to do justice according to their lights; but whose lights were often dim, and whose understandings were often harsh and narrow. He was powerfully built, with haughty, clear-cut features and dark complexion; and he always dressed with scrupulous care, in the rich costume then worn by the highest people in his native land. He had proved his courage on more than one stricken field; and he knew how to show both tact and firmness in dealing with his foes. But he was far less successful in dealing with his friends; and his imperious nature better fitted him to command a garrison than to rule over a settlement of Dutch freemen. It was inevitable that a man of his nature, who wished to act justly, but who was testy, passionate, and full of prejudices, should arouse much dislike and resentment in the breasts of the men over whom he held sway; and these feelings were greatly intensified by his invariably acting on the assumption that he knew best about their interests, and had absolute authority to decide upon them. He always proceeded on the theory that it was harmful to allow the colonists any real measure of self-government, and that what was given them was given as a matter of grace, not as an act of right. Hence, though he was a just man, of sternly upright character, he utterly failed to awaken in the hearts of the settlers any real loyalty to himself or to the government he represented; and they felt no desire to stand by him when he needed their help. He showed his temper in the first speech he made to the citizens, when he addressed them in the tone of an absolute ruler, and assured them that he would govern them "as a father does his children." Colonists from a land with traditions of freedom, put down in the midst of surroundings which quicken and strengthen beyond measure every impulse they may have in the direction of liberty, are of all human beings those least fitted to appreciate the benefits of even the best of paternal governments.

It was under Stuyvesant, in 1653, that the town was formally incorporated as a city, with its own local *schout* and its *schepens* and burgomasters, whose powers and duties answered roughly to those of both aldermen and justices. The schouts, schepens, and burgomasters together formed the legislative council of the city; and they also acted as judges, and saw to the execution of the laws. There was an advisory council as well.

The girls were wont to spread the house linen they had washed, and the path by which they walked thither gave its name to the street that is yet called Maiden Lane.

The struggling days of pioneer squalor were over, and New Amsterdam had taken on the look of a quaint little Dutch seaport town, with a touch of picturesqueness from its wild surroundings. As there was ever menace of attack, not only by the savages but by the New Englanders, the city needed a barrier for defence on the landward side; and so, on the present site of Wall Street, a high, strong stockade of upright timbers, with occasional blockhouses as bastions, stretched across the island. Where Canal Street now is, the settlers had dug a canal to connect the marshes on either side of the neck. There were many clear pools and rivulets of water; on the banks of one of them the girls were wont to spread the house linen they had washed, and the path by which they walked thither gave its name to the street that is yet called Maiden Lane. Manhattan Island was still, for the most part, a tangled wilderness. The wolves wrought such havoc among the cattle, as they grazed loose in the woods, that a special reward was given for their scalps, if taken on the island.

The hall of justice was in the stadt-huys, a great stone building, before which stood the high gallows whereon malefactors were executed. Stuyvesant's own roomy and picturesque house was likewise of stone, and was known far and near as the Whitehall, finally giving its name to the street on which it stood. The poorest people lived in huts on the outskirts; but the houses that lined the streets of the town itself were of neat and respectable appearance, being made of wood, their gable ends checkered with little black and yellow bricks, their roofs covered with tiles or shingles and surmounted by weathercocks, and the doors adorned with burnished brass knockers.

The shops, wherein were sold not only groceries, hardware, and the like, but also every kind of rich stuff brought from the wealthy cities of Holland, occupied generally the ground floors of the houses. There was a large, bare church, a good public-school house, and a great tavern, with neatly sanded floor, and heavy chairs and tables, the beds being made in cupboards in the thick walls; and here and there windmills thrust their arms into the air, while the half-moon of wharves jutted out into the river.

Stuyvesant's own roomy and picturesque house was known as the Whitehall, finally giving its name to the street on which it stood.

The houses of the rich were quaint and comfortable, with steeply sloping roofs and crow-step gables. A wide hall led through the middle, from door to door, with rooms on either side. Everything was solid and substantial, from the huge, canopied, four-post bedstead and the cumbrous cabinets, chairs, tables, stools, and settees, to the stores of massive silver plate, each piece a rich heirloom, engraved with the coat-of-arms of the owner. There were rugs on the floors, and curtains and leather hangings on the walls; and there were tall eight-day clocks, and stiff ancestral portraits. Clumsy carriages, and fat geldings to draw them, stood in a few of the stables; and the trim gardens were filled with shrubbery, fruit-trees, and a wealth of flowers, laid out in prim sweet-smelling beds, divided by neatly kept paths.

The poorer people were clad,—the men in blouses or in jackets, and in wide, baggy breeches; the women in bodices and short skirts. The schepens and other functionaries wore their black gowns of office. The gentry wore the same rich raiment as did their brethren of the Old World. Both ladies and gentlemen had clothes of every stuff and colour; the former, with their hair frizzed and powdered, and their persons bedecked with jewelry, their gowns open in front to show the rich petticoats, their feet thrust into high-heeled shoes, and with silk hoods instead of bonnets. The long coats of the gentlemen were finished with silver lace and silver buttons, as were their velvet doublets, and they wore knee-breeches, black silk stockings, and low shoes with silver buckles. They were fond of free and joyous living; they caroused often, drinking deeply and eating heavily; and the young men and maidens loved dancing parties, picnics, and long sleigh rides in winter. There were great festivals, as at Christmas and New Year's. On the latter day every man called on all his friends; and the former was then, as now, the chief day of the year for the children, devoted to the special service of Santa Claus.

Whenever the English and Dutch were at war, New Amsterdam was in a flutter over the always-dreaded attack of some English squadron. At last, in 1664, the blow really fell. There was peace at the time between the two nations; but this fact did not deter the England of the Stuarts from seizing so helpless a prize as the province of the New Netherlands. The English Government knew well how defenceless the country was; and the king and his ministers determined to take it by a sudden stroke of perfectly cold-blooded treachery, making all their preparations in secret, and meanwhile doing everything they could to deceive the friendly power at which the blow was aimed. Stuyvesant had continued without cessation to beseech the home government that he might be given the means to defend the province; but his appeals were unheeded by his profit-loving, money-getting superiors in Holland. He was left with insignificant defences, guarded by an utterly insufficient force of troops. The unblushing treachery and deceit by which the English took the city made the victory of small credit to them; but the Dutch, by their supine, short-sighted selfishness and greed, were put in an even less enviable light.

In September, 1664, three or four English frigates, and a force of several hundred land-troops under Col. Richard Nicolls suddenly appeared in the harbour. They were speedily joined by the levies of the already insurgent New Englanders of Long Island. Nicolls had an overpowering force, and was known to be a man of decision. He forthwith demanded the immediate surrender of the city and province. Stuyvesant wished to fight even against such odds; but the citizens refused to stand by him, and New Amsterdam passed into the hands of the English without a gun being fired in its defence.

New Amsterdam, now called New York, 1667.

1664-1674
New Amsterdam Becomes New York.
The Beginning of English Rule.

THE EXPEDITION against New Amsterdam had been organized with the Duke of York, afterward King James II., as its special patron, and the city was rechristened in his honour. To this day its name perpetuates the memory of the dull, cruel bigot with whose short reign came to a close the ignoble line of the Stuart kings.

Nicolls made the necessary changes with cautious slowness and tact. For nearly a year the city was suffered to retain its old form of government; then the schout, schepens, and burgomasters were changed for sheriff, aldermen, mayor, and justices. Vested rights were interfered with as little as possible; the patroons were turned into manorial lords; the Dutch and

Huguenots were allowed the free exercise of their religion; indeed, the feeling was so friendly that for some time the Anglican service was held in the Dutch Church in the afternoons. No attempt was made to interfere with the language or with the social and business customs and relations of the citizens. Nicolls showed himself far more liberal than Stuyvesant in questions of creed; and one of the first things he did was to allow the Lutherans to build a church and install therein a pastor of their own. He established a fairly good system of justice, including trial by jury, and practically granted the citizens a considerable measure of self-government. But the fact remained that the colony had not gained its freedom by changing its condition; it had simply exchanged the rule of a company for the rule of a duke. Nicolls himself nominated all the new officers of the city (choosing them from among both the Dutch and the English), and returning a polite but firm negative to the request of the citizens that they might themselves elect their representatives. He pursued the same course with the Puritan

Long Islanders; and the latter resented his action even more bitterly than did the Dutch.

However, his tact, generosity, and unfailing good temper, and the skill with which he kept order and secured prosperity endeared him to the colonists, even though they did at times just realize that there was an iron hand beneath the velvet glove. He completely pacified the Indians, who during his term of command remained almost absolutely tranquil, for the first time in a quarter of a century. He put down all criminals, and sternly repressed the licentiousness of his own soldiery, forcing them to behave well to the citizens. His honesty in financial matters was so great that he actually impoverished himself during his administration of the province. Meanwhile, the city flourished; for there was free trade with England and the English possessions, and even for some time a restricted right to trade with certain of the Dutch ports.

The colony had simply exchanged the rule of a company for the rule of a duke.

Nicolls soon wearied of his position, and sought leave to

resign; but he was too valuable a servant for the duke to permit this until the war with Holland, which had been largely brought on by the treacherous seizure of New Amsterdam, at length came to a close. The Peace of Breda left New York in the hands of the English; for the cold northern province, where now are States already far more populous than Holland, or than the England of that day, was then considered of less value than any one of half a dozen tropical colonies. On both sides the combatants warred for the purpose of getting possessions which should benefit their own pockets, not to found States of free men of their own race; they sought to establish trading-posts from whence to bring spices and jewels and precious metals, rather than to plant commonwealths of their children on the continents that were waiting to be conquered. The English were inclined to grumble, and the Dutch to rejoice, because the former

The English were inclined to grumble, and the Dutch to rejoice, because the former received New York rather than Surinam.

received New York rather than Surinam. As for Nicolls, when his hands were thus freed he returned home, having shown himself a warm friend to the colonists, especially the Dutch, who greatly mourned his going.

His successor was an archetypical cavalier named Francis Lovelace. He had stood loyally by the king in disaster and prosperity alike, and was a gallant, generous, and honest gentleman; but he possessed far less executive capacity than his predecessor. However, he trod in the footsteps of the latter so far as he could, and strove to advance the interests of the city in every way, and to conciliate the good-will of the inhabitants. He associated on intimate terms with the leading citizens, whether English, French, or Dutch, and established a social club which met at their different houses,—all three languages being spoken at the meetings. Being fond of racing, he gave prizes to be run for by swift horses on the Long Island race-course. Like his predecessor, his chief troubles were with the hard-headed and stiff-necked children of the Puritans on Long Island. When he attempted to tax them to build up the fort on Manhattan, they stoutly refused, and sent him an indignant protest; while on the other hand he was warmly supported by his Dutch and English councillors in New York. With the Indians he kept on good terms.

The city prospered under Lovelace as it had prospered under Nicolls. Its proprietor, the Duke of York, was a mean and foolish tyrant; but it was for his interest while he was not king to treat his colony well. Though an intolerant religious bigot, he yet became perforce an advocate of religious tolerance for New York, because his own creed, Roman Catholicism, was weak, and the hope of the feeble never rests in persecution. New York was thus permitted to grow in peace, and to take advantage of her great natural resources. Trade increased and ships were built; while in addition to commerce, many of the seafaring folk took to the cod and whale fisheries, which had just been started off the coasts. The whales were very plentiful, and indeed several were killed in the harbour itself. The merchants began to hold weekly meetings, thus laying the foundation for the New York

Exchange; and wealth increased among all classes, bringing comfort, and even some attempt at luxury, in its train.

This quick and steady growth in material prosperity was rudely checked by the fierce war which again broke out between England and Holland. Commerce was nearly paralyzed by the depredations of the privateers, and many of the merchants were brought to the verge of bankruptcy, while the public distress was

The merchants began to hold weekly meetings, thus laying the foundation for the New York Exchange.

widespread. It was known that the Dutch meditated an effort to recapture the city; and Lovelace made what preparations he could for defence. He busied himself greatly to establish a regular mail to Boston and Hartford, so that there might be overland communication with his eastern neighbours; and it was on one of his absences in New England that the city was recaptured by its former owners.

In July, 1673, a Dutch squadron under two grim old sea-dogs, Admirals Evertsen and Binckes, suddenly appeared in the lower bay. The English commander in the fort endeavoured to treat with them; but they would hearken to no terms save immediate surrender, saying that "they had come for their own, and their own they would have." The Dutch militia would not fight against their countrymen; and the other citizens were not inclined to run any risk in a contest that concerned them but little. Evertsen's frigates sailed up to within musket-shot of the fort, and firing began on both sides. After receiving a couple of broadsides which killed and wounded several of the garrison, the English flag was struck, and the fort was surrendered to the Dutch troops, who had already landed, under the command of Capt. Anthony Colve. So ended the first nine years of English supremacy at the mouth of the Hudson.

The victors at once proceeded to undo the work of the men they had ousted. Dutch was once more made the formal official language (though it had never been completely abandoned), and the whole scheme of the English government was overturned.

NEW YORK

This second period of Dutch supremacy on Manhattan Island lasted for but a year and a quarter. Then in November, 1674, the city was again given up to the English in accordance with the terms of peace between the belligerent powers, which provided for the mutual restitution of all conquered territory. With this second transfer New Amsterdam definitely assumed the name of New York; and the province became simply one of the English colonies in America, remaining such until, a century afterward, all those colonies combined to throw off the yoke of the mother country and become an independent nation.

Thus the province of the New Netherlands had been first taken by the English by an attack in time of peace, when no resistance could be made, and had been left in their possession because it was deemed of infinitely less consequence than such colonies as Java and Surinam; it had then been reconquered by the Dutch, in fair and open war, and had been again surrendered because of an agreement into which the home government was forced, owing to the phases which the European struggle had assumed. The citizens throughout these changes played but a secondary part, the fate of the city and province being decided, not by them, but by the ships and troops of Holland and England. Nor were the burghers as a whole seriously affected in their civil, religious, or social liberties by the changes. The Dutch and English doubtless suffered in turn from certain heartburnings and jealousies, as they alternately took the lead in managing the local government; but the grievances of the under-party were really mainly sentimental, for on the one hand no material discrimination was ever actually made against either element, and on the other hand the ruler for the time being, whether Dutch direcktor or English governor, always made both elements feel that compared to him they stood on a common plane of political inferiority.

Sir Edmund Andros was appointed by the English king as the governor who was to receive New York from the hands of Director Colve. This he did formally and in state, many courtesies being exchanged between the outgoing and incoming rulers; among the rest, Colve presented Andros with his own state-coach and the three horses that drew it. Andros at once reinstated the English form of government in both province and city, and once more, and this time finally, made the English the official language. New York was still considered as a proprietary colony of James; New Jersey was severed from it, and became a distinct province. The city itself, which had numbered some fifteen hundred inhabitants at the date of the original conquest from the Dutch, included about three thousand when English rule was for the second time established.

First watch house in New York, 1700.

1674-1720
New York Under the Stuarts.
The Growth of the Colonial Seaport.

ANDROS WAS a man of ability and energy, anxious to serve his master the duke, and also anxious to serve the duke's colony, in so far as its interests did not clash with those of the duke himself. He was of course a devoted adherent of the House of Stuart, an ardent royalist, and a believer in the divine right of kings, and in government by a limited ruling class, not by the great mass of the people governed. Yet, in spite of his imperious and fiery temper, he strove on the whole to do justice to the city of mixed nationalities over whose destinies he for the time being presided, and it throve well under his care. But though he tried to rule fairly, he made it distinctly understood that he, acting in the name of his over-lord the duke, was the real and supreme master. The city did not govern itself; for he appointed the mayor, aldermen, and other officers. Even some of his decrees which worked well for the city showed the arbitrary character of his rule, and illustrated the vicious system of monopolies and class and sectional

The middle-class citizens, Dutch and English alike, were bound together by the stubborn love of liberty.

legislation which then obtained. Thus he bestowed on New York the sole right to bolt and export flour. This trebled her wealth during the sixteen years that elapsed before it was repealed, but it of course caused great hardship to the inland towns. Unmixed good however resulted from his decree putting an end to the practice of holding Indians as slaves.

It might have been expected that after the conquest of New York the incoming English would have been divided by party lines from the Dutch, and that they would have been in strong alliance with their English neighbours to the eastward. The extreme royalist tone of the new government, and the anti-Puritan or Episcopal feeling of the most influential of the new settlers, were among the main causes which prevented either of these results from being brought about. The English Episcopalians and Royalists hated their sour, gloomy, fanatical countrymen of different belief much more bitterly than they did their well-to-do Dutch neighbours; and the middle-class citizens, Dutch and English alike, were bound together by ties of interest and by the stubborn love of liberty which was common to both races.

There was a succession of long wars with France, the New Yorkers, like the other English colonists, and like England herself, soon coming to look upon the French as their hereditary and natural foes. This continuous struggle with a powerful common enemy was a potent cause in keeping the colonists of Manhattan, like those of the rest of America, loyal to the mother country; and the growth of sentiments and interests hostile to the latter, though steady, was unappreciated even by the colonists themselves. Their internal politics were marked by unceasing struggles in the Assembly,—struggles, sometimes between the aristocratic and popular factions, sometimes between one or the other or both of these factions and whoever happened for the time to represent the Crown. The overthrow of the Stuart dynasty had resulted in an immense gain for liberty, and for free and orderly government in New York. The last Stuart king had never granted the liberties he had promised to the colonists; but by his successor they were immediately given in full. Hitherto New York's share in self-government had depended purely on the pleasure of her successive rulers. Under and owing to William of Orange, she made the first noteworthy advance in the direction of self-government by right, irrespective of the views of the royal governor who might be over her.

Throughout all this period New York was a little seaport town, without manufactures, and dependent upon ocean industries for her well-being. There was little inland commerce; everything was done by shipping. The merchants were engaged in the river trade with Albany and the interior, in the coast trade with the neighbouring colonies, in the fisheries, and in the sea trade with England, Africa, and the East and West Indies. Every few years there occurred a prolonged maritime war with either France or Spain, and sometimes with both. Then the seas were scourged and the coasts vexed by the war-ships and privateers of the hostile powers; and the intervals of peace were troubled by the ravages of pirate and picaroon. Commerce was not a merely peaceful calling; and those who went down to the sea in ships led troublous lives.

The seafaring folk, or those whose business was connected with theirs, formed the bulk of New York's white population. The poor man went to sea in the vessel the richer man built or owned or commanded; and where the one risked life and limb, the other at least risked his fortune and future.

New York was a little seaport town, without manufactures, and dependent upon ocean industries.

Many of the ventures were attended with great danger even in times of peace. Besides the common risks of storm and wreck, other and peculiar perils were braved by the ships that sailed for the Guinea Coast, to take part in the profitable but hideously brutal and revolting trade for slaves. The traffic with the strange coast cities of the Red Sea and the Indian Ocean likewise had dangers all its own. Pirate and sultan and savage chief had all to be guarded against, and sometimes outwitted, and sometimes outfought.

Moreover, the New York merchants and seamen were themselves ready enough to risk their lives and money in enterprises where the profits to be gained by peaceful trade came second, and those by legal warfare or illegal plundering first. In every war the people plunged into the business of privateering with immense zest and eagerness. New York Province dreaded the Canadians and Indians, but New York City feared only the fleets of France; her burghers warred, as well as traded, chiefly on the ocean. Privateering was a species of gambling which combined the certainty of exciting adventure with the chance of enormous profit, and it naturally possessed special attractions for the bolder and more reckless spirits. Many of the merchants who fitted out privateers lost heavily, but many others made prizes so rich that the profits of ordinary voyages sank into insignificance by comparison. Spanish treasure-ships, and French vessels laden with costly stuffs from the West Indies or the Orient, were brought into New York harbour again and again,—often after fights to the severity of which the battered hulls of both the captor and the vanquished vessel bore unequivocal testimony. When the prize was very rich and the crew of the privateer large, the home-coming of the latter meant a riot; for in such a case the flushed privateersmen celebrated their victory with wild orgies and outrages, and finally had to be put down by actual battle in the streets. The landowners were often merchants as well; and more than one of them was able to flank the gateway of his manor-house with the carved prows and figure-heads of the vessels his own privateers had captured.

In time of war both risk and profit were great, yet they were but little less in the short periods of peace, or rather of truce. Under the system of jealous trade-exclusion which then obtained, each trader was a possible smuggler, and the cruisers of every naval power were always harassing the merchantmen sailing under rival flags. Even if a vessel did not smuggle, she was liable at any moment to be seized on the pretext that she was trying to; and so, as she had to undergo the dangers in any event, she felt no reluctance in attempting to gather the profits when occasion offered. Again, the line dividing the work of the privateer from the work of the pirate was easy to overstep, and those who employed the one were not reluctant at times to profit by the deeds of the other. At Madagascar there was a regular fort and station to which some of the New York merchants sent ships for the sole purpose of trading with the pirate vessels who carried their ill-gotten goods thither. Many a daring skipper who obeyed the law fairly well in Atlantic waters, felt free to do as he wished when he neared Madagascar, or cruised through the Red Sea and the Indian Ocean. The rich cargoes of oriental goods, the spices, perfumes, silks, shawls, rugs, pearls, and golden coin and jewels, were of such value that men did not care to ask too closely how they were acquired. There were plenty of adventurous young New Yorkers, of good blood, who were themselves privateersmen, Red-Sea men, or slavers; and in the throng of seafaring men of this type, the crews and captains of the pirate ships passed unchallenged. The taverns and low houses along the water-front of the little seaport were filled with wind-roughened sailor-folk, outlandish in speech and dress, wild of look, black of heart, and ripe for any desperate venture. Their dare-devil commanders were not only tolerated but welcomed as guests at the houses of many among the gentry and merchants, who had themselves in one way or another gained

There was a suggestion of hazardous fortunes, ill made and lightly lost.

great profit from lawless ocean warfare. Their mad freaks and furious orgies and carouses made them the terror of quiet people; but their lavish extravagance with their stores of strange Spanish, Indian, and Arabian coin gave them also a certain popularity.

The goods brought from the far eastern lands by these men, and by their fellow sea-rovers of slightly stricter morality, gave a touch of quaint luxury, and their own presence added an air of dash and adventure, to the life of the growing town on Manhattan Island. There was a suggestion of the Orient and of hazardous fortunes, ill made and lightly lost, in the costly goods with which the rich burghers and manorial lords decked their roomy houses, and clothed themselves and their wives. The dress of the time was picturesque; and the small social world of New York, as haughty and exclusive after its own fashion as any, looked leniently on the men whose deeds made it possible for the titled Crown officials, and the untitled leaders of the local oligarchy, alike, to go clad in rich raiment. More than one sea-chief of doubtful antecedents held his head high among the New York people of position, on the infrequent occasions when he landed to revel and live at ease, while his black-hulled, rakish craft was discharging her cargo at the wharves, or refitting for another mysterious voyage. The grim-visaged pirate captain, in his laced cap, rich jacket, and short white knee-trunks, with heavy gold chains round his neck, and jewel-hilted dagger in belt, was a striking and characteristic feature of New York life at the close of the seventeenth century. Soon afterward the boldness and the serious nature of the piratical ravages thoroughly roused the home government, which made resolute efforts to stop them. The colonial authorities joined to hunt the rovers from their coasts; and though the men of the black flag continued to ply their trade in tropical seas, they never after that time appeared in the colonial seaports save by stealth.

After a couple of years of practical interregnum, New York received another governor, one Robert Hunter, whose term lasted until 1720. He was a wise and upright man, who did justice to all, though, if anything, favouring the popular party. But the personality of the governor was rapidly becoming of less and less consequence to New York as the city and province grew in size. The condition of the colony and the policy of the British King and Parliament were the really important factors of the problem.

About this time there was a great influx of Germans from the Rhine provinces. They were poor peasants who had fled from before the French armies; and while most went on into the country, a considerable number remained in New York, to add one more to the many elements in its population. As they were ignorant and poverty-stricken, the colonists of English, Dutch, and Huguenot blood looked down on and despised them, not wholly without reason.

> *One feature of the settlement of America is that each mass of immigrants feels much distrust and contempt for the mass which comes a generation later.*

One feature of the settlement of America is that each mass of immigrants feels much distrust and contempt for the mass—usually of a different nationality—which comes a generation later. Presbyterians from Scotland and Ireland began to straggle in, were allowed to build a church, and got a firm foothold.

The city was growing slowly. English, Dutch, and Huguenot names succeeded one another in the mayoralty, showing that there was no attempt on the part of one race to exclude the others from their share of political power. The mass of the people were not very well off, and grudged taxes; the annual expenditure of the city government was only about £300 and was covered by the annual income. The Assembly was already dabbling in paper money, and it had been found necessary to pass poor-laws, and authorize the arrest of street beggars.

Burn's coffee house (front), 1760.

1720-1764
The Close of the Colonial Period.

IN 1710 New York City contained some 6,000 inhabitants, in 1750 over 12,000, and at the outbreak of the Revolution about 20,000. It was a smaller town than either Boston or Philadelphia, with a society far less democratic, and divided by much sharper lines of caste. Strangers complained, then as now, that it was difficult to say what a typical New Yorker was, because New York's population was composed of various races, differing widely in blood, religion, and conditions of life. In fact, this diversity has always been the dominant note of New York. No sooner has one set of varying elements been fused together than another stream has been poured into the crucible. There probably has been no period in the city's growth during which the New Yorkers whose parents were born in New York formed the majority of the population; and there never has been a time when the bulk of the citizens were of English blood.

All this is in striking contrast to what has gone on in some other American cities, as, for instance, Boston. Colonial Boston was a Puritan English town, where the people were in all essentials wonderfully like one another. New York, however, never was really an English town, and its citizens always differed radically among themselves in morals, manners, and physical well-being, no less than in speech, blood, and creed. From time to time new ethnic elements have made their appearance, but the change has been not from one race to another, but from one mixture of races to another.

Of course there are very sharp points of contrast other than those of mere size and growth between colonial New York and the New York of the United States. The three leading religious denominations of the present United States had but small and scanty followings in colonial times. In New York, just prior to the Revolution, the Methodists and Baptists had but a small meeting-house apiece, and the handful of Catholics no recognized place of worship whatever; whereas at the present day the Methodists and Baptists form the two leading and characteristic denominations in the country districts of America, while Catholicism has forged to the front in the cities.

In eighteenth-century New York both the Quakers and Jews had places of worship. The Germans had one Lutheran and one Calvinistic Church; but the German pre-revolutionary immigrants did not produce many men of note, and their congregations remained small and unprogressive, their young men of spirit drifting off to other churches as they learned English. The Presbyterian congregations, on the other hand, throve apace, in spite of the petty and irritating persecution of the Episcopalians. They received many

New York never was really an English town, and its citizens always differed radically among themselves.

recruits from the Scotch and Scotch-Irish immigrants; and to a man they were all zealous upholders of popular rights, and truculently defiant toward Great Britain. The Irish of that day were already a prominent element of New York life; but they were Presbyterians, not Catholics. They celebrated Saint

Patrick's day with enthusiasm, and their toasts to Ireland and America, together with their scarcely veiled hostility to England, would not be out of place on similar occasions at present; but some of their other toasts, such as those to the memory of King William and to the Protestant succession, would scarcely appeal to a Milesian patriot nowadays.

The Huguenots were assimilated more easily than any other element of the population, and produced on the whole the highest grade of citizens. By the middle of the century the Hollanders likewise had begun to speak English. It was the official language of the colony, and the young men of push, who wished to make their mark in the world, had to learn it in order to succeed. The conservative men, the sticklers for old ways and customs, clung obstinately to Dutch; and the consequence was that the energetic young people began to leave the Dutch churches, and to join the Episcopalian and Presbyterian congregations in constantly increasing numbers,— doing exactly what we see being done by the Scandinavian and German Lutherans in portions of the Northwest at the present day. The drain was so serious that in 1764, as the only means of putting a stop thereto, it was decided to hold the church services in both English and Dutch; and forty years afterward Dutch was entirely abandoned. These measures arrested the decay of the Dutch Reformed Church, and prevented its sharing the fate of total extinction which befell the Swedish Lutheran bodies on the Delaware; but they were not taken in time to prevent the church from falling much behind the place which it should have occupied, taking into account the numbers, intelligence, and morality of its members,—for throughout the colonial period the Dutch remained the largest of the many elements in New York's population.

As the wealthy Dutch and Huguenot families assimilated themselves to the English, they intermarried with them, and in many cases joined the Episcopal Church; though a considerable number, especially among those whose affiliations were with the popular party, remained attached to one or the other of the Calvinist bodies. The Episcopal Church—or, as it was then the Church of England—was the fashionable organization, the one to which the Crown officials belonged, and the centre round which the court party rallied. Among its members were to be found most of the influential people,—the manorial lords and large merchants, who controlled the affairs of the colony, and were the social and political leaders. It claimed to be in a sense the State Church, and had many immunities and privileges; and as far as it could, though only in petty fashion, it oppressed the dissenting bodies,—notably the Presbyterians, who were not, like the Huguenots and Hollanders, protected by treaty. When King's College, now Columbia, was founded by the colony, it was put under the control of the Church of England, and was made in a small way a seat of Tory feeling. The various Protestant bodies were all filled with sour jealousy of one another, and were only united in cordial hatred of the Romanists, to whom they forbade entrance into the colony; and though they tolerated the presence of the Jews, they would not for some time let them vote.

Social lines were very strongly marked,—the intensely aristocratic make-up of the town being in striking contrast to the democratic equality typical of a young American city of the same size nowadays. The manorial lords stood first in rank and influence, and in the respect universally accorded them. They lived at ease in the roomy mansions on their great tenant-farmed estates; and they also usually owned fine houses in either New York or Albany, and sometimes in both. Their houses were really extremely comfortable, and were built with a certain stately simplicity of style which contrasted very favourably with the mean or pretentious architecture of most New York buildings dating back to the early or middle portions of the present century. They were filled with many rooms, wherein a host of kinsmen, friends, and retainers might dwell; and they had great halls, broad verandas, heavy mahogany-railed staircases, and huge open fireplaces, which in winter were crammed with roaring logs. The furniture was handsome, but stiff and heavy; the books were few; and there were masses of silver plate on the sideboards of the large dining-rooms. The gentry carried swords, and dressed in the artificial, picturesque fashion of the English upper classes; whereas the commonalty went about their work in smocks or leather aprons. Near Trinity Church was the "mall," or promenade for the fashionable set of the little colonial town. By an unwritten law none but the members of the ruling class used it; and on fine afternoons it was filled with a gayly dressed throng of young men and pretty girls, the latter attended by their negro waiting-maids.

They were never permitted by their English friends to forget that they were nothing but provincials.

Prominent in the crowd, were the scarlet coats of the officers from the English regiments, constantly quartered in New York because of the recurring French wars. The owners of these coats moved with an air of easy metropolitan superiority, a certain insolently patronizing condescension, which always awakened both the admiration and the jealous anger of the provincial aristocrats.[1] The leading colonial families stood on the same social plane with the English country gentlemen of wealth, and were often connected by marriage with the English nobility; but they could never forget—and were never permitted by their English friends to forget—that after all they were nothing but provincials, and

---

[1] European travellers naturally enough often failed to understand the aristocratic constitution of the New York social and governmental systems. The local aristocrats seemed to them uncouth and provincial; they were struck by the fact that they were often engaged in trade or other occupations which gentlemen were forbidden to enter by the European social code; and they saw that it was, of course, much easier than in the Old World for a man of

that provincials could not stand quite on an equality with the old-world people.

The New York gentry, both of town and country, were fond of horse-racing, and kept many well-bred horses. They drove out in chariots or huge clumsy coaches with their coats of arms blazoned on the panels,—the ship of the Livingstons, the lance of the De Lanceys, the burning castle of the Morrises, and the other armorial bearings of the families of note being known to all men throughout the province. On a journey the gentry either went by water in their own sloops or else in these coaches, with liveried postilions and outriders; and when one of the manorial lords came to town, his approach always caused much excitement, the negroes, children, and white work-people gathering to gaze at the lumbering, handsomely painted coach, drawn by four huge Flemish horses, the owner sitting inside with powdered wig and cocked hat, scarlet or somber velvet coat, and silver-hilted sword. In the town itself

energy to rise from the lowest to the highest round of the social ladder, no matter what his origin was. The aristocracy existed nevertheless. So to a London noble, Squire Western seemed only a boor, and he cordially hated all lords in return; yet Squire Western and his fellows formed at home a true oligarchy. And the constitution of the rude country society in which he lived was as emphatically aristocratic as was that of the capital of England.

sedan chairs were in common use. There was a little theatre where performances were given, now by a company of professional actors, and again by the officers of the garrison regiments; and to these performances as well as to the balls and other merry-makings the ladies sometimes went in chariots or sedan chairs and sometimes on their own daintily-shod feet. The people of note usually sent their negro servants, each dressed in the livery of his master, in advance to secure good seats. There was much dancing and frolicking, besides formal dinners and picnics; sailing parties, and in winter skating parties and long sleigh rides were favourite amusements; all classes took part eagerly in the shooting matches. The dinners were rather heavy entertainments, with much solemn toast-drinking; and they often ended with boisterous conviviality,— for most of the men drank hard, and prided themselves on their wine cellars. Christmas and New Year's day were great festivals, the latter being observed in Dutch fashion,—the gentlemen calling at all the houses of their acquaintance, where they feasted and drank wine. Another Dutch festival of universal observance was Pinkster, held in the spring-tide. It grew to be especially the negroes' day, all of the blacks of the city and neighbouring country gathering to celebrate it. There was a great fair, with merry-making and games of all kinds on the Common, where the City Hall park now is; while the whites also assembled to look on, and sometimes to take part in the fun. Most of the house servants were negro slaves.

The people of means sometimes had their children educated at home, and sometimes sent them to the little colleges which have since become Columbia and Princeton,— colleges which were then inferior to a good English grammar school. Occasionally the very wealthy and ambitious sent their boys to Oxford or Cambridge, where the improved opportunities for learning were far more than counter-balanced by the fact that the boy was likely to come back much less fitted than his home-staying brother to play a man's part in the actual work of American life. The true colonial habit of thought, the deference for whatever came from the home country, whether rank or title, fashion or learning, was nearly universal, although the bolder and more independent spirits were already beginning to assume an attitude of protest against it. In truth it was very easy to get opinions ready made from the Old World, while it was hard work to fashion them out originally from the raw material ready at hand in the New. New Yorkers had as yet been given little opportunity for deep thought or weighty action. Provincial politics offered but a cramped and narrow field for vigorous intellects; and to the native New Yorker, war held no higher possibilities than the leadership in a dashing foray against the Canadians and Indians, or the captaincy in a successful cruise among French and Spanish merchantmen. There was no home literature worthy of the name, and little chance for its immediate development; and art was not much better off.

The New York merchants and smaller landed proprietors stood next to the great manorial families; they mixed with them socially, and often married among them, following their lead in matters political. The merchants lived in comfortable brick or stone houses, and owned large warehouses and stores of every description. Many of them had great gardens round their homes; for New York was still but a little country town. Nevertheless, as the years went by, its growth, sluggish at first, became more and more rapid. Coffee-houses were started; there were good inns for the wealthy, and taverns for the poorer; and there were schools, a poor-house, and a jail.

Next to the merchants came the middle class,—the small freeholders with whom the suffrage stopped short. They were the rank and file of the voters, and in political contests generally followed the banner of one or the other of the great families, from whom they were separated by a deep social gulf. Then came the class of free workmen; and below these,— though as years went by, merging into them,—the very distinct class of unfree whites, the imported bond-servants, redemptioners, apprentices, and convicts,

There was no home literature worthy of the name, and little chance for its immediate development; and art was not much better off.

who had been sent to the colonies. These were by no means all criminals and paupers, though very many such were included among them. Some were honest, poor men, who could not get a living at home, and had no money wherewith to go abroad; and these were regularly sold for a term of years to make good

their passage money. They were of many nationalities,—
English, Irish, and Germans predominating, though there were
some Scotch, Welsh, and Swiss. On the arrival of a ship
containing them, they were usually duly advertised, the
occupation—as tradesman, farmer, or labourer—for which they
were best fitted being specified, and were then immediately
sold at auction into what was simply slavery for a limited
period; and as they were sometimes harshly treated they were
very prone to run away. Judging by the advertisements in the
colonial newspapers the runaway white bond-servants were
almost as numerous as the runaway slaves. After their term of
service was over, some of them became honest, hard-working
citizens, while the others swelled the ranks of the idle, vicious,
semi-criminal class, clustering in the outskirts and alleys of the
town. As a whole, this species of immigrant was very harmful,
and added a most undesirable element to the population. It
may well be doubted if relatively to our total numbers, we have
had any class of immigrants during the present century which
as a class was so bad; and indeed it is safe to say that in
proportion, eighteenth-century New York had quite as much

vice and vicious poverty within its limits as the present huge city; and most of the vice and poverty among the whites was due to this importation of bond-servants and convicts.

The first newspaper published in the city was a small weekly, started in 1725, under the name of the "New York Gazette." It was the organ of the governor and aristocratic or court party. Nine years later a rival appeared in the shape of the "Weekly Journal," edited by a German immigrant named Zenger, and from the start avowedly the organ of the popular party. The royal governor at the time was a very foolish person named Cosby, appointed on the theory which then obtained, to the effect that a colonial governorship was to be used as a place for pensioning off any court favourite otherwise unprovided for, without reference to the result of his appointment upon the colony. He possessed a genius for petty oppression, which marked him for the especial hatred of the people. Zenger published a constant succession of lampoons, ballads, and attacks on all the Crown officials, the governing class, and finally even on Cosby himself. He was arrested and thrown into jail on the charge of libel; and the trial, which occupied most of the summer of 1735, attracted great attention. The chief-justice at the time was one of the Morrises, who belonged to the popular party; and as he was suspected of leaning to Zenger's side, he was turned out of office and replaced by one of the De Lanceys, the stoutest upholders of the Crown. De Lancey went to the length of disbarring Zenger's lawyers, so that he had to be defended by one imported from Philadelphia. But the people at large made Zenger's cause their own, and stood by him resolutely; while every ounce of possible pressure and influence from the Crown officials was brought to bear against him. The defence was that the statements asserted to be libellous were true. The attorney-general for the Crown took the ground that if true the libel was only so much the greater. The judges instructed the jury that this was the law; but the jury refused to be bound, and acquitted Zenger. The acquittal, which definitely secured the complete liberty of the press, was hailed with clamourous joy by the mass of the population; and it gave an immense impetus to the growth of the spirit of independence. From this time on, the two parties were much more sharply defined than before. The court party, the faction of the Crown officials and of the bulk of the local aristocracy, included most of the Episcopalians and many of the Hollanders and Huguenots, while the rest of the population, including the Presbyterians, formed the popular party. The former often styled themselves Tories, and the latter Whigs, in imitation of the two English parties. Each faction was under the leadership of a number of the great landed families; for even in the ranks of the popular party the voters still paid reverence to the rich and powerful manorial lords. These great families were all connected by marriage, and were all split up by bitter feuds and political jealousies. The De Lanceys held the headship of the court, and the Livingstons of the popular party; and the contest took on so strongly personal a colour that these two families almost gave their names to the factions with which they were respectively identified as leaders.

Fraunces' Tavern, 1777.

1764-1774
The Unrest Before the Revolution.

NO SOONER was the long succession of French wars closed by the conquest of Canada, than American history entered on a new stage. Hitherto the contests had been waged between European powers for the possession of the various colonies, both the interests and the efforts of these colonies being of secondary importance. From this time on, however, the American settlements became themselves the chief factors in solving the problems of their own future, and the questions of policy hinged on the issues between them and the mother country.

In every colony outside of New England and Virginia there was a large Tory party; and nowhere was it relatively larger than in New York. The peculiarly aristocratic structure of New York society had a very great effect upon the revolutionary movement, which took on a two-fold character, being a struggle for America against England on the one hand, and an uprising of the democracy against the local oligarchy on the other. The lowest classes of the population cared but little for the principles of either party; and sided with one or the other accordingly as their temporary interests or local feuds and jealousies influenced them. They furnished to both Whigs and Tories the scoundrels who hung in the wake of the organized armies, hot for plunder and murder,—the marauders who carried on a ferocious predatory warfare between the lines or on the Indian frontier, and who took advantage of the general disorder to wreak their private spites and rob and outrage the timid, well-to-do people of both sides, with impartial brutality. A large number of the citizens, possibly nearly half, were but lukewarm adherents of either cause. Among them were many of the men

The peculiarly aristocratic structure of New York society had a very great effect upon the revolutionary movement.

of means, who were anxious to side with the winners, and feared much to lose their possessions, and a still greater number of men who were too indifferent and cold-hearted, too deficient in patriotism and political morality to care how the affair was decided. Among them were many men also who were of ultra-conservative mind, not yet far enough advanced in that difficult school which teaches how to combine a high standard of personal liberty with a high standard of public order. The bulk of the intelligent working-classes, the most truly American members of the colonial body politic, formed also the bulk of the popular party. Here also all the Presbyterians and the majority of the members of the Dutch Reformed and Huguenot congregations naturally found their proper place. Very many of the gentry also belonged to it; and it was led by some of the great families,—the Livingstons, Schuylers, and others,—including all those whose pride of caste was offset by their belief in freedom, or was overcome by their profound Americanism, when caste and country came into conflict. Most of the Episcopalian clergy and the majority of their flocks, as well as minority of the Dutch Reformed congregations, belonged to the court party, as did the greater portion of the local aristocracy, led by the De Lanceys, De Peysters, and Philippses, and by the Johnsons, who ruled the Mohawk Valley in half-savage, half-feudal state.

Of course the lines between these various classes were not drawn sharply at the outset. In the beginning very few, even of the most violent extremists among the Whigs dared to hint at independence; while scarcely any of the most bigoted Tories upheld the Crown and the Parliament in all their doings. The power lay in the hands of the moderate men, who did not wish for extreme measures, until the repeated blunders and aggressions of the king and his advisers exasperated the people at large beyond the possibility of restraint. The ablest and purest leaders of the New York patriots during the Revolution—men like Schuyler, Jay, Morris, and Hamilton— disliked mob-violence as much as they hated tyranny, and felt no sympathy with the extremists of their own party. An English statesman like Chatham, or an English statesman like Walpole, might have held these men, and therefore the American colonies, to their allegiance. But the necessary breadth and liberality were lacking, possibly in the temper of the age itself, certainly in the temper of King George and his ministers. They persevered in their course, offering concessions only when the time they would have been accepted was past. Then the break came, and the moderate men had to choose the side with which they wished to range themselves; and after some misgivings most of them—and the best of them—put love of their country above loyalty to their king, and threw in their lot with the revolutionary party. However, not a few of the leading families divided, sending sons into both camps.

When in 1765 the Stamp Act was passed by the British Parliament, the popular party held the control of the New York legislature. Accordingly, among all the colonial legislatures New York's stood foremost in stout assertion of the right of the colonies to the full enjoyment of liberty, and in protest against taxation without representation. The New York newspapers were especially fervid in denouncing the law, while the legislature appointed a committee to correspond concerning the subject with the legislative bodies of the other colonies. Finally the Stamp Act Congress met in New York, nine of the thirteen colonies being represented, and voted a Declaration of Rights and an Address to the King. But the people themselves, acting through the suddenly raised, and often secret or semi-secret, organizations, took more effective measures of protest than either congress or legislature. The most influential of these societies was that styled the "Sons of Liberty;" all of them were raised in the first place with an excellent purpose, and numbered in their ranks many stanch and wise patriots, but like all such organizations they tended to pass under the control of men whose violence better fitted them to raise mobs than to carry through a great revolution.

After the repeal of the Stamp Act, the colonies were not again stirred by a common emotion until the passage by Parliament of the Tea Act, avowedly passed, and avowedly resisted simply to test the principle of taxation. Its enactment was the signal for the Sons of Liberty and other societies—such as that of the Mohawks—to reorganize at once. In Philadelphia, New York, and Boston, the sentiment was unanimous that the tea shipped from England should be thrown overboard or shipped back; and Boston was the first to put the threat into execution. New York followed suit in April 1774, when the first tea ships reached the harbour, only to be boarded by an excited multitude who heaved the tea-chests of one vessel into the harbour, and forced the other to stand out to sea without landing her cargo.

The measures of retaliation against Boston taken by the British government, aroused in New York the liveliest sympathy for the New Englanders. The radical party, acting without any authority through a self-constituted Committee of Vigilance, began to correspond with the Boston extremists; and this gave alarm to the moderate men, who at once aroused themselves and took the matter into their own hands, so as not

The measures of retaliation against Boston taken by the British government, aroused in New York the liveliest sympathy.

to be compromised by unwise and hasty action. Accordingly, to the chagrin of the extremists, they promptly disowned and repudiated the action of the vigilance committee. At the same time they thoroughly distrusted the zeal of their aristocratic legislature. They therefore convoked a meeting of the freeholders, who with due solemnity elected a Committee of Fifty-one to correspond with the other colonies. This committee was entirely in the hands of the moderate men, even containing in its ranks several Tories and very few of the radicals, and did a piece of work of which it is difficult to over-estimate the importance; for it was the first authoritatively to suggest the idea of holding the first Continental Congress. This suggestion is said to have been adopted by the advice of John Jay, a young lawyer of good Huguenot family. Under the auspices of the committee the freeholders chose five delegates to this congress,—including John Jay, and as a matter of course, one of the Livingstons also. The radicals and extremists, the Sons of Liberty and the old Committee of Vigilance, with the Committee of Mechanics—the body supposed to represent most nearly the unenfranchised classes—were greatly discontented with the moderate measures of the Committee of Fifty-one; and there was very nearly a rupture between the two wings of the patriot party. By mutual concessions this was averted; and the delegates were elected without opposition. They took their full part in the acts of the first Continental Congress during its short session, the colony being thereby committed to the common cause. At the same time, when the Committee of Fifty-one went out of existence its place was taken by another, differing in little more than the fact of having sixty members.

Gov. George Clinton's house, Pearl Street, 1775.

1775-1783
The Revolutionary War.

THE YEAR 1775 was for New York City one of great doubt and anxiety. All classes had united in sending delegates to the first Continental Congress. The most ardent supporters of the Crown and Parliament were opposed to the Stamp Act and Tea Act, and were anxious to protest against them, and to try to bring about a more satisfactory understanding between the mother country and her colonies. On the other hand the popular party as yet shrank from independence. The men who thus early thought of separation from Britain were in a small and powerless minority; indeed, they were but a little knot of republican enthusiasts, who for several years had been accustomed at their drinking-bouts to toast the memory of the famous English regicides.

With the summoning of the second Continental Congress this unity disappeared, as the Whigs and Tories began to drift in opposite ways,—the one party toward violent measures with separation in the background, the other toward reconciliation even at the cost of submission. A Tory mob tried to break up the meeting at which delegates to the second Congress were chosen, and were only driven off after a number of heads had been broken.

New York still remained doubtful. In fact, all of the colonies outside of Virginia and New England—although containing strong patriot parties, animated by the most fiery zeal—were as a whole somewhat lukewarm in the Revolution, for they contained also large Tory, and still larger neutral elements in their midst. If left to themselves it is even doubtful if at this precise time they would have revolted; they were pushed into independence by the Virginians and New Englanders. Not only was the Tory element in New York very large, but there was also a powerful body of Whigs—typified by Schuyler and Gouverneur Morris—who furnished very able soldiers and statesmen when the actual fighting broke out, but who were thoroughly disgusted by the antics of the city mob; and though the major portion of this mob was rabidly anti-British as far as noise went, it was far more anxious to maltreat unhappy individual Tories than to provoke a life and death struggle with the troops and war-ships of the British king. Nor must it be forgotten that there were plenty of Tories in the mob itself, and these among the most abandoned and violent of the city's population.

The provincial legislature was as a body actively loyal to the king. But, in spite of the presence of the large Tory and neutral elements, the revolutionary party was unquestionably in the lead among the people, and contained the most daring spirits and the loftiest minds of the colony. There is much to admire in the resolute devotion which many tens of thousands of Loyalists showed to the king, whose cause they made their own; and there is much to condemn in the excesses committed by a portion of the popular party. Nevertheless, as in the great English civil war of the preceding century, the party of liberty was the party of right. The purest and ablest New Yorkers were to be found in the ranks of the revolutionists; for keen-eyed and right thinking men saw that on the main issue justice was with the colonists. The young men of ardent, generous temper, such as Alexander Hamilton, John Jay and Gouverneur Morris, found it impossible to side with the foreign party. They were Americans, freemen, conscious that they deserved to stand on a level with the best of any land; and they could not cast in their lot with the party which held as a cardinal point of its creed the doctrine of their inferiority.

The purest and ablest New Yorkers were to be found in the ranks of the revolutionists.

The mass of quiet, good, respectable people, of conservative instincts and rather dull feelings, might rest content with being treated as inferiors, if on the whole they were treated well; might submit to being always patronized and often bullied, if only they were protected; might feel they owed an honest debt of gratitude to their champions in former wars; and might shrink from enduring the hundred actual evils of civil conflict merely for the sake of protesting against the violation of certain abstract rights and principles; but the high-spirited young men, the leaders in thought and action, fixed with unerring certainty upon the central and vital truth of the situation. They saw that the struggle, when resolved into its ultimate elements, was to allow Americans the chance for full and free development, uncramped by the galling sense of admitted inferiority. The material benefits conferred by the continuance of British rule might or might not offset the material disadvantages it involved; but they could not weigh against the evils of a system which dwarfed the character and intellect,—a system which condemned all colonists to remain forever in the second rank, which forbade their striving for the world's great prizes, unless they renounced their American birthright, and which deprived them of those hopes that especially render life worth living in the eyes of the daring and ambitious. To their free, bold spirits, the mere assumption of their inferiority was an intolerable grievance, as indeed it has ever been esteemed by the master races of the world. Sooner than submit, in ignoble peace and safety, to an order of things which would have stunted the moral and mental growth of the country, they were willing to risk not only the dangers of war with the British king, but the far worse dangers of disorder, violence, anarchy, and a general loosening of the social bonds among Americans themselves. The event proved their wisdom.

Yet the dangers were very real and great. The country was still in the gristle; the thews had not hardened. There had been much lawlessness, in one quarter and another, already; and the long struggle of the Revolution produced hideous disorganization. It is impossible to paint in too dark colours the ferocity of the struggle between the Whigs and Tories; and the patriot mobs, either of their own accord or instigated by the Sons of Liberty and kindred bodies, often took part in proceedings which were thoroughly disgraceful. New York had her full share of these mob-outbreaks during the summer of 1775. The lawyers, pamphleteers, and newspaper writers, who contributed so largely to arouse the people, also too often joined to hound the populace on to the committal of outrages. The mob broke into and plundered the houses of wealthy Loyalists, rode Tories on rails, or tarred, feathered, and otherwise brutally maltreated them, and utterly refused to allow to others the liberty of speech and thought they so vociferously demanded for themselves. They hated and threatened the Episcopalian, or Church of England, clergy, because of that part of the liturgy in which the king was prayed for; and finally the Episcopalian churches had to be closed for fear of them. They drove off the Tory president of King's (now Columbia) College, and joined with a Connecticut mob to wreck the office of the Loyalist newspaper. It is to their credit, however, that there was little

There had been much lawlessness, and the long struggle of the Revolution produced hideous disorganization.

interference with the courts of justice. They did not come into collision with the soldiers of the garrison, and the latter were permitted to embark for Massachusetts Bay, where hostilities had fairly begun; but they refused to allow any stores or munitions of war to be shipped to the beleaguered garrison at Boston. There were frequent rows with the boats' crews of the frigates in the bay; once with the result of a broadside being fired into the town by an affronted man-of-war.

In spite of these disturbances, New York still remained reluctant to burn her boats, and throw in her lot once for all with the patriots. Both Washington, on his way to take command of the American army at Boston, and Tryon, the royal governor, were received with the same formal tokens of respect. Meanwhile business was at a standstill, and a third of the inhabitants had left the town.

By the beginning of the year 1776 the real leaders of the city and province, the men of mark, and of proved courage and capacity, saw that all hope of compromise was over. They had been disgusted with the turbulence of the mob, and the noisy bragging and threatening of its leaders,—for the most part frothy men, like Isaac Sears, who sank out of ken when the days of rioting passed, and the grim, weary, bloody years of fighting were ushered in; but they were infinitely more disgusted with the spirit of tyrannous folly shown by the King and Parliament. The only possible outcome was independence.

The citizens had become thoroughly hostile to the Tory Colonial Assembly, and had formally set it aside and replaced it, first by a succession of committees, and then by a series of

---

[2] The names of the members of these committees and provincial congresses are English, Dutch, Huguenot, Scotch, Irish, and German; the English in the lead, with the Dutch coming next. Many of the families were represented by more than one individual: thus of

provincial congresses, corresponding to the central Continental Congress. The mob never controlled these congresses, whose leaders were men like Schuyler, Van Zandt, Van Cortlandt, Jay, the Livingstons, the Morrises, the Van Rensselaers, the Ludlows,—representatives of the foremost families of the New York gentry.[2] When the Provincial Congress, with unanimity and the heartiest enthusiasm, ratified the Declaration of Independence, it was evident that the best men in New York were on the Revolutionary side.

In January, 1776, Washington sent one of his generals to take command in New York, and in April he himself made it his headquarters, having at last driven the enemy from Boston. Soon the motley levies of the patriot army were thronging the streets,—some in homespun or buckskin, a few in the dingy scarlet they had worn in the last French war, Marylanders in green hunting-shirts, Virginians in white smocks, militia in divers uniforms from the other colonies, and Washington's guards, the nucleus of the famous Continental troops of the

the Livingstons there were Walter, Peter Van Brugh, Robert L., and Philip; of the Ludlows, Gabriel and William; of the Beekmans, David and William; of the Roosevelts, Isaac and Nicholas; etc.

line, in their blue and buff. All New York was in a ferment; and the ardent young patriots were busy from morning till night in arming, equipping, and drilling the regiments that made up her quota.[3]

The city was in no state to resist a siege, or an attack by a superior force. Her forts, such as they were, would not have availed against any foe more formidable than a light frigate or heavy privateer. The truth was that the United States—for such the revolted colonies had become—were extremely vulnerable to assault. Their settled territory lay in a narrow belt, stretching for a thousand miles along the coast. Its breadth was but a hundred miles or so, in most places; then it faded off, the inland frontier lying vaguely in the vast, melancholy, Indian-haunted forests. The ferocious and unending warfare with the red woodland tribes kept the thinly scattered pioneers busy defending their own hearthstones, and gave them but scant breathing spells in which to come to the help of their brethren in the old settled regions. The eastern frontier was the coast-

---

[3] The younger men among the leading city families furnished most of the captains for the city regiments,—among them being Henry S. Livingston, Abraham Van Wyck, John Berrian, John J. Roosevelt, and others. Many of the most distinguished, however, had themselves risen from the ranks.

line itself, which was indented by countless sounds, bays, and harbours, and here and there broken by great estuaries or tide-water rivers, which could carry hostile fleets into the heart of the land. The bulk of the population, and all the chief towns, lay in easy striking distance from the sea. Almost all the intercolonial trade went along the water-ways, either up and down the rivers, or skirting the coast. There was no important fortress or fortified city; no stronghold of note. A war power having command of the seas possessed the most enormous advantage. It menaced the home trade almost as much as the foreign, threatened the whole exposed coast-line,—and therefore the settled country which lay alongside it,—could concentrate its forces wherever it wished, and could penetrate the country at will. The revolted colonists had no navy, while the mother country possessed the most powerful in the world. She was fourfold their superior in population, and a hundred-fold in wealth; she had a powerful standing army, while they had none. Moreover, the colonists' worst foes were those of their own household. The active Tories and half-hearted neutrals formed the majority of the population in many districts,—including Long Island and Staten Island. The Americans were then a race of yeomen, or small farmers, who

The Americans were then a race of yeomen, or small farmers, who were both warlike in temper and unmilitary in habits.

were both warlike in temper and unmilitary in habits. They were shrewd, brave, patriotic, stout of heart and body, and proudly self-reliant, but impatient of discipline, and most unwilling to learn the necessity of obedience. Their notion of war was to enlist for a short campaign, usually after the hay was in, and to return home by winter, or sooner, if their commanding officers displeased them. They seemed unable to appreciate the need of sustained effort. The jealousies of the different States and their poverty and short-sighted parsimony, the looseness of the Federal tie, the consequent impotence of the central government, and the radical unfitness of the Continental Congress as a body to conduct war, all combined to render the prospects of the patriots gloomy. Only the heroic grandeur of Washington could have built up victory from these jarring elements.

It was therefore natural for the patriot party of New York to look before it leaped; but the leap once taken, it never faltered. No other State north of South Carolina was so harried by the forces of the king; and against no other State did they direct such efforts or send such armies,—armies which held portions of it to the close of the war. Yet the patriot party remained firm throughout, never flinching through the long years, cheering the faint-hearted, crushing out the Tories, and facing the enemy with unshaken front.

Early in the summer a great armament began to gather in the lower bay; a force more numerous and more formidable than the famous Armada which nearly two centuries before had sailed from Spain against England. Scores of war-ships of every kind, from the heavy liner, with her tiers of massive cannon, to the cutter armed with a couple of light cannon, and hundreds of transports and provision-ships began to arrive, squadron by squadron. Aboard them was an army of nearly forty thousand fighting-men. A considerable number were Hessians, and other German troops, hired out by the greedy and murderous

baseness of the princelets of Germany. The Americans grew
to feel a peculiar hatred for these Hessians, because of the
ravages they committed, and because of the merely
mercenary nature of their services; but the wrong lay not with
the poor, dull-witted, hard-fighting boors, but with their
sordid and contemptible masters.

With the near approach of this great army the Tories
began plotting; and most rigorous measures were taken to
stamp out these plots. For some reason the lower class of
liquor sellers were mostly Tories, and many of the plots were
found to have their origin among them or their customers.
The Loyalist gentry had for the most part fled to the British
lines. Those who remained behind—including both the
mayor and ex-mayor of the city—were forced to take a
stringent oath of allegiance to the Continental Congress and
the new nation. The Tory plots were not mythical; one was
unearthed which aimed at nothing less than the abducting or
killing of Washington,—the ring leader, Thomas Hickey, an
Irish soldier who had deserted from the royal army, being
hanged for his villany.

Washington saw the hopelessness of trying to defend New York with the materials he had, against such a force as was coming against it; and it was proposed to burn the town and retire so that the king's troops might gain nothing by the capture. This was undoubtedly the proper course to follow, from a purely military standpoint; but the political objections to its adoption were insuperable. Washington laboured unceasingly at the almost hopeless task of perfecting the discipline of his raw, ill-armed, ill-provided, jealousy-riven army; and he put down outrages, where he could, with a heavy hand. Nevertheless, many

It was proposed to burn the town so that the king's troops might gain nothing by the capture.

of the soldiers plundered right and left, treating the property of all Loyalists as rightfully to be confiscated, and often showing small scruple in robbing wealthy Whigs under pretence of mistaking them for Tories.

At last, in mid-August, the British general, Lord Howe, made up his mind to strike at the doomed city. He landed on Long Island a body of fifteen or twenty thousand soldiers,—

English, Irish, and German.[4] The American forces on the island were not over half as numerous, and were stationed in the neighbourhood of Brooklyn. Some of the British frigates had already ascended the Hudson to the Tappan Sea, and had cannonaded the town as they dropped down stream again, producing a great panic, but doing little damage. The royal army was landed on the 22d; but Lord Howe, a very slow, easy-going man, did not deliver his blow until five days later. The attack was made in three divisions, early in the morning, and was completely successful. The Americans permitted themselves to be surprised, and were out-generalled in every way. Not half the force on either side was engaged. Some of the American troops made but a short stand; others showed a desperate but disorderly valour. About two thousand of them were killed, wounded, or captured, principally the latter; while the British loss was less than four hundred, the battle being won without difficulty. Howe seemingly had the remainder of the American army completely at his mercy, for it was cooped

---

[4] It is a curious fact that in the Revolutionary War the Germans and Catholic Irish should have furnished the bulk of the auxiliaries to the regular English soldiers; for as the English is the leading strain in our blood, so the German and the Irish elements come next. The Maryland

up on a point of land which projected into the water. But he felt so sure of his prey that he did not strike at once; and while he lingered and made ready, Washington, who had crossed over to the scene of disaster, perfected his plans, and by a masterly stroke ferried the beaten army across to New York during the night of the 29th. The following morning the king's generals woke to find that their quarry had slipped away from them.

The discouragement and despondency of the Americans were very great, Washington almost alone keeping up heart. It was resolved to evacuate New York; the chief opponent of the evacuation being General George Clinton, a hard-fighting soldier from Ulster county, where his people of Anglo-Irish origin stood well, having intermarried with the Tappans and De Witts of the old Dutch stock. Clinton did not belong to the old colonial families of weight, being almost the only New York Revolutionary leader of note who did not; and in consequence they rather looked down on him, while he in turn repaid their

Catholics, and most of the German settlers, were stout adherents of the Revolutionary cause. The fiercest and most ardent Americans of all, however, were the Presbyterian Irish settlers and their descendants.

dislike with interest. He was a harsh, narrow-minded man, of obstinate courage and considerable executive capacity, very ambitious, and a fanatical leader of the popular party in the contest with the Crown.

On September 15, Howe, having as usual lost a valuable fortnight by delay, moved against Manhattan Island. His troops landed at Kip's Bay, where the Americans opposed to them, mostly militia, broke in disgraceful panic and fled before them. Washington spurred to the scene in a frenzy of rage, and did his best to stop the rout, striking the fugitives with his sword, and hurling at them words of bitter scorn; but it was all in vain, the flight could not be stayed, and Washington himself was only saved from death or capture by his *aides-de-camp*, who seized his bridle-reins and forced him from the field.

However, Washington's acts and words had their effect, and as the Americans recovered from their panic they became heartily ashamed of themselves. The king's troops acted with such slowness that the American divisions south of Kip's Bay were able to march past them unmolested. These divisions, on their retreat, were guided by a brilliant young officer, Aaron Burr, then an *aide-de-camp* to the rough, simple-hearted old wolf-killer General Putnam; and the rear was protected by Alexander Hamilton and his company of New York artillerymen, who in one or two slight skirmishes beat off the advance guard of the pursuers.

Washington drew up his army on Haarlem Heights, and the next day inflicted a smart check on the enemy. An American outpost was attacked and driven in by the English light troops, who were then themselves attacked and roughly handled by the Connecticut men and Virginians. They were saved from destruction by some regiments of Hessians and Highlanders; but further reinforcements for the Americans arrived, and the royal troops were finally driven from the field. About a hundred Americans and nearly three times as many of their foes were killed or wounded. It was nothing more than a severe skirmish; but it was a victory, and it did much to put the Americans in heart.

Besides, it was a lesson to the king's troops, and made Howe even more cautious than usual. For an entire month he remained fronting Washington's lines, which, he asserted, were too strong to be carried by assault. Then the rough sea-dogs of the fleet came to his rescue, with the usual daring and success of British seamen. His frigates burst through the obstructions which the Americans had fondly hoped would bar the Hudson, and sailed up past the flanks of the patriot army; while the passage to the Sound was also forced. Washington had no alternative but to retreat, which he did slowly, skirmishing heavily. At White Plains, Howe drove in the American outposts, suffering more loss than he inflicted. But a fortnight later, in mid-November, a heavy disaster befell the Americans. In deference to the wishes of Congress, Washington had kept garrisons in the two forts which had been built to guard the Hudson, and Howe attacked them with sudden energy. One was evacuated at the last moment; the other was carried by assault, and its garrison of nearly three thousand men captured, after a resistance which could not be called more than respectable. Washington retreated into New Jersey with his dwindling army of but little more than three thousand men. The militia had all left him long before; and his short-term "regular" troops also went off by companies and regiments as their periods of enlistment drew to a close; and the stoutest friends of America despaired. Then, in the icy winter, Washington suddenly turned on his foes, crossed the Delaware, and by the victory of Trenton, won at the darkest moment of the war, re-established the patriot cause.

For the next seven years, New York suffered all the humiliations that fall to the lot of a conquered city. The king's troops held it as a garrison town, under military rule, and made it the headquarters of their power in America. Their foraging parties and small expeditionary columns ravaged the neighbouring counties, not only of New York, but of New Jersey and Connecticut. The country in the immediate vicinity of the city was overawed by the formidable garrison and remained Loyalist; beyond this came a wide zone or neutral belt where the light

The king's troops held it as a garrison town, under military rule, and made it the headquarters of their power in America.

troops and irregular forces of both sides fought one another and harried the wretched inhabitants. Privateers were fitted out to cruise against the shipping of the other States,

The soldiers looted the small public libraries, hawking the books about the streets, or exchanging them for liquor in the low saloons.

precisely as the privateers of the patriots had sailed from the harbour against the shipping of Britain in the earlier days of the war.

Most of the active patriots among the townsfolk had left the city; only the poor and the faint-hearted remained behind, together with the large Tory element, and the still larger portion of the population which strove to remain neutral in the conflict. This last division contained the only persons whose conduct must be regarded as thoroughly despicable. Emphatically the highest meed of praise belongs to the resolute, high-minded, far-seeing men of the patriot party,—as distinguished from the mere demagogues and mob leaders who, of course, are to be found associated with every great popular movement. We can also heartily respect the honest and gallant Loyalists who sacrificed all by their devotion to the king's cause. But the selfish time-servers, the timid men, and those who halt between two burdens, and can never make up their minds which side to support in any great political crisis, are only worthy of contempt.

The king's troops were not cruel conquerors; but they were insolent and overbearing, and sometimes brutal. The Loyalists were in a thoroughly false position. They had drawn the sword against their countrymen; and yet they could not hope to be treated as equals by those for whom they were fighting. They soon found to their bitter chagrin that their haughty allies regarded them as inferiors, and despised an American Tory almost as much as they hated an American Whig. The native army had not behaved well in the half-Tory city of New York; but the invading army which drove it out behaved much worse. The soldiers broke into and looted the corporation, the college, and the small public libraries, hawking the books about the streets, or exchanging them for liquor in the low saloons. They also sacked the Presbyterian, Dutch Reformed, and Huguenot churches, which were later turned into prisons for the captured Americans; while on the other hand, the Episcopalian churches, which had been closed owing to the riotous conduct of the patriot mob, were re-opened. The hangers-on of the army,—the camp-followers, loose women, and the like,—formed a regular banditti, who infested the streets after dark, and made all outgoings dangerous. There was a completely organized system of gigantic jobbery and swindling, by which the contractors and commissaries, and not a few of the king's officers as well, were enriched at the expense of the British government; and when they plundered the government wholesale, it was not to be supposed that they would spare Tories. The rich Royalists, besides of course all the Whigs, had their portable property, their horses, provisions, and silver taken from them right and left,—sometimes by bands of marauding soldiers, sometimes by the commissaries, but always without redress or compensation, their representations to the officers in command being scornfully disregarded. They complained in their bitter anger that the troops sent to reconquer America seemed bent on campaigning less against the rebels than against the king's own friends and the king's own army-chest. Many of the troops lived at free quarters in the private houses, behaving well or ill according to their individual characters.

A few days after New York was captured it took fire, and a large portion of it was burnt up before the flames were checked. The British soldiers were infuriated by the belief that the fire was the work of rebel incendiaries, and in the disorganization of the day they cut loose from the control of their officers and committed gross outrages, bayoneting a number of men, both Whigs and Tories, whom on the spur of the moment they accused of being privy to the plot for burning the city. Two or three years afterward there was another great fire, which consumed much of what the first had spared.

On the day of this first fire an American spy, Nathan Hale, was captured. His fate attracted much attention on account of his high personal character. He was a captain in the patriot army, a graduate of Yale, and betrothed to a beautiful girl; and he had volunteered for the dangerous task from the highest sense of duty. He was hanged the following morning, and met his death with quiet, unflinching firmness, his last words expressing his regret that he had but one life to lose for his country. He was mourned by his American comrades as deeply and sincerely and with to the full as much reason as a few years later André was mourned by the officers of the king.

Four or five thousand American soldiers were captured in the battles attending the taking of New York; and thenceforward the city was made the prison-house of all the captured patriots. The old City Hall, the old sugar-house of the Livingstons (a gloomy stone building, five stories high, with deep narrow windows), and most of the non-Episcopal churches were turned into jails, and packed full of prisoners. It was a much rougher age than the present; the prisons of the most civilized countries were scandalous even in peace, and of course prisoners of war fared horribly. The king's

> *Five thousand soldiers were captured in the battles attending the taking of New York; the city was made the prison-house of all the captured patriots.*

officers as a whole doubtless meant to behave humanely; but the provost-marshal of New York was a very brutal man, and the cheating commissaries who undertook to feed the prisoners made large fortunes by furnishing them with spoiled provisions, curtailing their rations, and the like. The captives were huddled together in ragged, emaciated, vermin-covered and fever-stricken masses; while disease, bad food, bad water, the cold of winter, and the stifling heat of summer ravaged their squalid ranks. Every morning the death-carts drew up at the doors to receive the bodies of those who during the night had died on the filthy straw of which they made their beds. The prison-ships were even worse. They were evil, pestilent hulks of merchantmen or men-of-war, moored mostly in Wallabout Bay; and in their noisome rotten holds men died by hundreds, and were buried in shallow pits at the water's edge, the graves being soon uncovered by the tide. In after years many hogsheads of human bones were taken from the foul ooze to receive christian burial.

So for seven dreary years New York lay in thraldom, while Washington and his Continentals battled for the freedom of America. Nor did Washington battle only with the actual foe in the field. He had to strive also with the short-sighted and sour jealousies of the different States, the mixed impotence and intrigue of Congress, the poverty of the people, the bankruptcy of the government, the lukewarm timidity of many, the open disaffection of not a few, and the jobbery of speculators who were sometimes to be found high in the ranks of the army itself. Moreover, he had to contend with the general dislike of discipline and sustained exertion natural to the race of shrewd, brave, hardy farmers whom he led,—unused as they were to all restraint, and unable to fully appreciate the necessity of making sacrifices in the present for the sake of the future. But his soul rose above disaster, misfortune, and suffering; he had the heart of the people really with him, he was backed by a group of great statesmen, and he had won the unfaltering and devoted trust of the band of veteran soldiers with whom he had achieved victory, suffered defeat, and wrested victory from defeat for so many years; and he triumphed in the end.

On November 25, 1783, the armies of the king left the city they had held so long, carrying with them some twelve thousand Loyalists; while on the same day Washington marched in with his troops and with the civil authorities of the State.

Trinity Church, 1791.

1783-1800
The Federalist City.

NEW YORK was indeed a dreary city when the king's troops left it after their sojourn of seven years. The spaces desolated by the great fires had never been built up, but still remained covered with the charred, melancholy ruins; the churches had been dismantled, the houses rifled. Business was gone, and the channels in which it had run were filled up. The Americans on taking possession once more had to begin all over again. They set busily to work to rebuild the fallen fortunes of the town; but the destruction had been so complete, and the difficulties in the way of getting a fair start were so great, that for four years very little progress was made. Then affairs took a turn for the better; the city began to flourish as it never had flourished before, and grew in wealth and population at a steadily increasing pace.

The dismantled churches were put in order; and Trinity, which had been burnt down in the fire of 1776, was entirely rebuilt. King's College had its name changed to Columbia, and was again started, the first scholar being De Witt Clinton, a nephew of George Clinton, at the time governor of the State. The free public library—the New York Society Library—was revived on a very much larger scale, and a good building erected, wherein to house the books. The new constitution of the independent State of New York completely did away with the religious disabilities enforced under the old provincial government, and declared and maintained absolute religious toleration and equality before the law. In consequence a Catholic church was soon built; while the Methodists increased rapidly in numbers and influence.

It was during this period of the foundation of the Federal government, and during the immediately succeeding period of the supremacy of the Federalists in national affairs that New York City played its greatest and most honourable part in the government of the nation. Never before or since has it occupied so high a position politically, compared to the country at large; for during these years it was the seat of power of the brilliant Federalist party of New York State. Alexander Hamilton, John Jay, and at the end of the time Gouverneur Morris, lived in the city, or so near it as to have practically the weight and influence of citizens; and it was the home likewise of their arch-foe Aaron Burr, the prototype of the skilful, unscrupulous ward-politician, so conspicuous in the later periods of the city's development.

It was during this period that New York City played its greatest and most honourable part in the government of the nation.

Hamilton, the most brilliant American statesman who ever lived, possessing the loftiest and keenest intellect of his time, was of course easily the foremost champion in the ranks of the New York Federalists; second to him came Jay, pure, strong and healthy in heart, body, and mind. Both of them watched with uneasy alarm the rapid drift toward anarchy; and both put forth all their efforts to stem the tide. They were of course too great men to fall in with the views of those whose antagonism to tyranny made them averse from order. They had little sympathy with the violent prejudices produced by the war. In particular they abhorred the vindictive laws directed against the persons and property of Tories; and they had the manliness to come forward as the defenders of the helpless and excessively unpopular Loyalists. They put a stop to the wrongs which were being inflicted on these men, and finally succeeded in having them restored to legal equality with other citizens, standing up with generous fearlessness against the clamour of the mob.

As soon as the project for a closer union of the States was broached, Hamilton and Jay took it up with ardour. New York City followed their lead, but the State as a whole was against them. The most popular man within its bounds was stout old Governor Clinton, and he led the opposition to the proposed union. Clinton was a man of great strength of character, a good soldier, and stanch patriot in the Revolutionary War. He was bitterly obstinate and prejudiced, and a sincere friend of popular rights. He felt genuine distrust of any form of strong government. He was also doubtless influenced in his opposition to the proposed change by meaner motives. He was the greatest man in New York; but he could not hope ever to be one of the greatest in the nation. He was the ruler of a small sovereign State, the commander-in-chief of its little army, the admiral of its petty navy, the leader of its politicians; and he did not wish to sacrifice the importance that all of this conferred upon him. The cold, suspicious temper of the small country freeholders, and the narrow jealousy they felt for their neighbours, gave him excellent material on which to work.

Nevertheless, Hamilton won, thanks to the loyalty with which New York City stood by him. By untiring effort and masterful oratory he persuaded the State to send three delegates to the Federal constitutional convention. He himself went as one, and bore a prominent part in the debates; his two colleagues, a couple of anti-Federalist nobodies, early leaving him. He then came back to the city where he wrote and published, jointly with Madison and Jay, a series of letters, afterward gathered into a volume called "The Federalist,"—a book which ranks among the ablest and best which have ever been written on politics and government. These articles had a profound effect on the public mind. Finally he crowned his labours by going as a representative from the city to the State convention, and winning from a hostile body a reluctant ratification of the Federal constitution.

The townsmen were quicker witted, and politically more far-sighted and less narrow-minded than the average country folk of that day. The artisans, mechanics, and merchants of New York were enthusiastically in favour of the Federal constitution, and regarded Hamilton as their especial champion. To assist him and the cause they planned a monster procession, while the State convention was still sitting. Almost every representative body in the city took part in it. A troop of light horse in showy uniforms led, preceded by a band of trumpeters and a light battery. Then came a personator of Columbus, on horseback, surrounded by woodsmen with axes,—the axe being pre-eminently the tool and weapon of the

American pioneer. Then came farmers in farmers' dress, driving horses and oxen yoked to both plough and harrow, while a new modelled threshing-machine followed. The Society of the Cincinnati came next. The trades followed: gardeners in green aprons, tailors, grain-measurers, bakers, with a huge "Federal loaf" on a platform drawn by ten bay horses; brewers, and coopers, with a stage drawn by four horses, bearing the "Federal cask," which the workmen finished as the procession moved, butchers, tanners, glovers, furriers, carpenters, masons, bricklayers, whitesmiths, blacksmiths, cordwainers, peruke-makers, florists, cabinet-makers, ivory-turners, shipwrights, riggers, and representatives of scores of other trades. In every part of the procession fluttered banners with Hamilton's figure and name, and the great feature of the show was the Federal ship "Hamilton," drawn by ten horses. It was a thirty-two-gun frigate in miniature, twenty-seven feet long, fully rigged, and manned by thirty seamen and marines. Thirteen guns from her deck gave the signal to start, and saluted at times during the procession. The faculty and students of the University, the learned societies and professions, the merchants, and distinguished strangers brought up the rear. The procession moved out to the Bayard House, beyond the city, where a feast for six thousand people was served.

For the first year of government under the new constitution, New York was the Federal capital. It was thither

New York has always been pre-eminently a career open to talent.

that Washington journeyed to be inaugurated President with stately solemnity, April 30, 1789. The city had by this time fully recovered its prosperity; and when it became the headquarters for the ablest statesmen from all parts of the Union, its social life naturally became most attractive, and lost its provincial spirit. However, its term of glory as the capital was short, for when Congress adjourned in August, 1790, it was to meet at Philadelphia.

The political history of the city during the twelve years of Washington's and Adams's administrations, is the history of a nearly balanced struggle between the Federalists and the anti-

Federalists, who gradually adopted the name, first of Republicans and then of Democrats. As always in our political annals, individuals were constantly changing sides, often in large numbers; but as a whole, party continuity was well preserved. The men who had favoured the adoption of the constitution grew into the Federal party; the men who had opposed it, and wished to construe it as narrowly as possible, and to restrict the powers of the central government even to the point of impotence, became Jeffersonian Republicans.

Hamilton and Jay were the heart of the Federalist party in the city and State. Both were typical New Yorkers of their time,—being of course the very highest examples of the type, for they were men of singularly noble and lofty character. Both were of mixed and non-English blood, Jay being of Huguenot and Hollander stock, and Hamilton of Scotch and French creole. Hamilton, born out of New York, was in some ways a more characteristic New Yorker than Jay; for New York, like the French Revolution, has always been pre-eminently a career open to talent. The distinguishing feature of the city has been its broad liberality; it throws the doors of every career wide open to all adopted citizens.

Jay lacked Hamilton's brilliant audacity and genius; but he possessed an austere purity and poise of character which his greater companion did not. He was twice elected governor of the State, serving from 1795 to 1801; indeed, he was really elected to the position in 1792, but was cheated out of it by most gross and flagrant election frauds, carried on in Clinton's interest, and connived at by him. His popularity was only temporarily interrupted even by the storm of silly and unwarranted abuse with which New York City, like the rest of the country, greeted the successful treaty which he negotiated when special envoy to England in 1794.

Hamilton was, of course, the leader of his party. But his qualities, admirably though they fitted him for the giant tasks of constructive statesmanship with which he successfully grappled, did not qualify him for party leadership. He was too impatient and dictatorial, too heedless of the small arts and unwearied, intelligent industry of the party manager. In fighting for the adoption of the constitution he had been heartily supported by the great families,—the Livingstons, the Van Rensselaers, and his own kin by marriage, the Schuylers. Afterward he was made secretary of the treasury, and Jay chief-justice, while through his efforts Schuyler and Rufus King—a New York City man of New England origin—were made senators. Chancellor Robert R. Livingston was not an extreme believer in the ideas of Hamilton. He was also jealous of him, being a very ambitious man, and was offended at being, as he conceived, slighted in the distribution of the favours of the national administration. Accordingly, he deserted to the Republicans with all his very influential family following. This was the first big break in the Federalist ranks.

When Washington was inaugurated President he found that he had a number of appointments to make in New York. Almost all the men he thus appointed were members of the party that had urged the adoption of the Constitution,—for Washington, though incapable of the bitter and unreasoning partisanship which puts party above the public welfare and

morality, was much more of a party man than it has been the
fashion to represent him, and during the final years of his life,
in particular, was a strong Federalist. Clinton distributed the
much larger and more important State patronage chiefly
among his anti-Federalist adherents. There was then no
patronage at all in the hands of the local, that is, the county
and city, authorities; for though an immense amount was given
to the mayor, he was really a State official.

The parties were very evenly matched in New York City, no
less than in the State at large, during the closing twelve years
of the century,—the period of Federalist supremacy in the
nation. The city was the pivotal part of the State, and the great
fighting-ground. It was carried alternately by the Federalists
and Democrats, again and again. Aaron Burr, polished, adroit,
unscrupulous, was the most powerful of the city Democracy.
He was elected to the United States Senate to succeed
Schuyler, and was in turn himself succeeded by Schuyler.
Hamilton grew to regard him with especial dislike and
distrust, because of his soaring ambition, his cunning, and his

lack of conscience. The Livingstons backed him ardently
against the Federalists, and one of their number was elected
and re-elected to Congress from the city.
De Witt Clinton was also forging to the
front, and was a candidate for State
office from the city on more than one
occasion, sharing in the defeats and
victories of his party. Jay's two successive
victories, on the other hand, gave the

Aaron Burr, polished, adroit, unscrupulous, was the most powerful of the city Democracy.

Federalists the governorship of the State for six years. Under
Hamilton's lead they won in New York City rather more often
than they lost. In 1799 they gained a complete victory, utterly
defeating the Democratic ticket, which was headed by Burr;
and the legislature thus chosen elected the Federalist
Gouverneur Morris to the United States Senate. The
newspapers reviled their opponents with the utmost
bitterness, and often with ferocious scurrility. The leading
Federalist editor in the city was the famous dictionary-maker,
Noah Webster.

Party and personal feeling was intensely bitter all through these contests. Duels were frequent among the leaders, and riots not much less so among their followers. The mob turned out joyfully, on mischief bent, whenever there was any excuse for it; and the habit of holding open-air meetings, to denounce some particular person or measure, gave ample opportunity for outbreaks. At these meetings, speakers of the for-the-moment unpopular party were often rather roughly handled,—a proceeding which nowadays would be condemned by even the most heated partisans as against the rules of fair play. The anti-Federalists, at some of their public meetings, held to denounce the adoption of the Constitution, or to break up the gatherings of those who supported it, got up regular riots against their opponents. At one of the meetings, held for the purpose of denouncing Jay's treaty with England,—a treaty which was of great benefit to the country, and the best that could then have been negotiated,—Hamilton was himself maltreated.

At the approach of the Presidential election of 1800, Burr

took the lead in organizing the forces of the Democracy. He was himself his party's candidate for the Vice-Presidency; and he managed the campaign with consummate skill. As before, the city was the pivotal part of the State, while the State's influence in the election at large proved to be decisive. The Democracy of the city was tending to divide into three factions. The Clintons were the natural leaders; but the Livingston family was very powerful, and was connected by marriage with such men as James Duane, a city politician of great weight, and Morgan Lewis, afterward governor; and both the Clintonians and Livingstons, jealous of one another, were united in distrust of Burr. Accordingly, the latter dexterously managed to get up a combination ticket containing the names of the most prominent members of each faction. This secured him against any disaffection. He then devoted himself to the work of organization. By his tact, address, and singular personal charm, he had gathered round him a devoted band of henchmen, mostly active and energetic young men. He made out complete lists of all the voters, and endeavoured to find out how each group could be reached and influenced, and he told off every worker to the district where he could do most good.

As so often since in this city, the statesman, the man of mark in the national arena, went down before the skilful ward-politician.

He was indefatigable in getting up ward meetings also. Hamilton fought him desperately, and with far greater eloquence, and he was on the right side; but Hamilton was a statesman rather than a politician. He had quarreled uselessly with some of the greatest men in his own party; and he could not devote his mind to the mastery of the petty political detail and intrigue in which Burr revelled. Burr won the day by a majority of five hundred votes. As so often since in this city, the statesman, the man of mark in the national arena, went down before the skilful ward-politician.

Thus the great Federalist party fell from power, not to regain it, save in local spasms here and there. It was a party of many faults,—above all the one unforgivable fault of distrusting the people,—but it was the party which founded our government, and ever most jealously cherished the national honour and integrity. New York City has never produced any other political leaders deserving to rank with the group of distinguished Federalists who came from within, or from just without, her borders. She has never since stood so high politically, either absolutely, or relatively to the rest of the country.

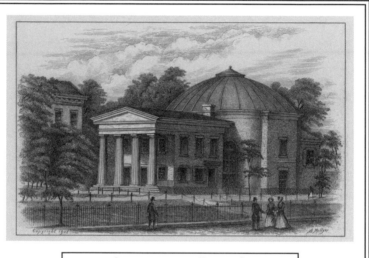

Rotunda in City Hall Park, 1816.

1801-1821
The Beginning of Democratic Rule.

AT THE beginning of the century, New York was a town of sixty thousand inhabitants. The social life was still aristocratic. The great families yet retained their prestige. Indeed, the Livingstons were at the zenith of their power in the State, and possessed enormous influence, socially and politically. They were very wealthy, and lived in much state, with crowds of liveried negro servants, free and slave. Their city houses were large and handsome, and their great country-seats dotted the beautiful banks of the Hudson.

The divisions between the upper, middle, and lower classes were sharply marked. The old families formed a rather exclusive circle, and among them the large landowners still claimed the lead, though the rich merchants, who were of similar ancestry, much outnumbered them, and stood practically on the same plane. But the days of this social and political aristocracy were numbered. They lost their political power first, being swamped in the rising democratic tide; and their social primacy—mere emptiness when thus left unsupported—followed suit a generation or so later, when their descendants were gradually ousted even from this last barren rock of refuge by those whose fathers or grandfathers had, out of the humblest beginnings, made their own huge fortunes. The fall of this class, as a class, was not to be regretted; for its individual members did not share the general fate unless they themselves deserved to fall. The descendant of any old family who was worth his salt, still had as fair a chance as any one else to make his way in the world of politics, of business, or of literature; and according to our code and standard, the man who asks more is a craven.

However, the presence of the great families undoubtedly gave a pleasant flavour to the gay social life of New York during the early years of the century. It had a certain half-provincial dignity of its own. The gentlemen still dressed, with formal and elaborate care, in the costume then worn by the European upper classes,—a costume certainly much more picturesque, if less comfortable, than that of the present day. The ladies were more apt to follow the fashions of Paris than of London. All well-to-do persons kept their own heavy carriages, and often used them for journeys no less than for pleasure drives. The social season was at its height in the winter, when there was an uninterrupted succession of dinners, balls, tea-parties, and card-parties. One of the great attractions was the Park Theatre, capable of holding twelve hundred persons, and always thronged when there was a good play on the boards. Large sleighing-parties were among the favourite pastimes, dinner being taken at some one of the half-dozen noted taverns a few miles without the city, while the drive back was made by torchlight if there was no moon. Marriages were scenes of great festivity. In summer the fashionable promenade was the Battery Park, with its rows and clumps of shade-trees, and broad walk by the

The social season was at its height in the winter, when there was an uninterrupted succession of dinners, balls, tea-parties, and card-parties.

water; and on still nights there was music played in boats on the water. The "gardens"—such as Columbia Gardens, and

There were thirty-odd churches; and the two principal streets or roads were Broadway and the Bowery.

Mt. Vernon Gardens[5] on Broadway—were also meeting-places in hot weather. They were enclosed pieces of open ground, covered with trees, from which coloured lanterns hung in festoons. There were fountains in the middle, and little tables at which ice-cream was served. Round the edges were boxes and stalls, sometimes in tiers; and there was usually a fine orchestra. When the hot months approached, the custom was to go to some fashionable watering-place, such as Ballston Springs, where the gaiety went on unchecked.

The houses of the well-to-do were generally of brick, and those of the poorer people of wood. There were thirty-odd churches; and the two principal streets or roads were Broadway and the Bowery. After nightfall the streets were lighted with oil lamps; each householder was obliged to keep the part of the

---

[5] This was at Leonard Street, then "a little out of town."

thoroughfare in front of his own house clean swept. There were large markets for vegetables, fruits, and meat, brought in by the neighbouring farmers, and for fish and game,—Long Island furnishing abundance of venison, and of prairie fowl, or, as they were then called, heath hens. Hickory wood was generally used for fuel; the big chimneys being cleaned by negro sweep boys. Milk was carried from house to house in great cans, by men with wooden yokes across their shoulders. The well-water was very bad; and pure spring-water from without the city was hawked about the streets in carts, and sold by the gallon.

The sanitary condition of the city was very bad. A considerable foreign immigration had begun,—though a mere trickle compared to what has come in since,—and these immigrants, especially the Irish, lived in cellars and miserable hovels. Every few years the city was scourged by a pestilence of yellow fever. Then every citizen who could, left town; and among those who remained, the death rate ran up far into the hundreds.

As the city grew, the class of poor who were unable, at least in times of stress, to support themselves, grew likewise; and organized charities were started in the effort to cope with the evil. Orphan asylums and hospitals were built. Societies for visiting the poor in their homes were started, and did active work,—and by their very existence showed how much New York already differed from the typical American country district or village, where there were few so poor as to need such relief, and hardly any who would not have resented it as an insult. As early as 1798 one society reported that it had supported through a hard winter succeeding a summer of unusual sickness, over three hundred widows and orphans who would otherwise have had to take refuge in the almshouse. It goes without saying, however, that this acute poverty was always local and temporary; there was then no opportunity for the pauperism and misery of overcrowded tenement-house districts.

The first savings-bank was established in 1816. The foundations of our free-school system were laid in 1805. The Dutch had supported schools at the public expense during their time of supremacy; but after their government was overturned, the schooling had been left to private effort. Every church had its own school, learning being still the special property of the clergy; and there were plenty of private schools and charity free schools in addition. Public-spirited citizens, however, felt that in a popular government the first duty of the State was to see that the children of its citizens were trained as they should be. Accordingly, a number of prominent citizens organized themselves into a society to establish a free school, obtained a charter from the legislature, and opened their school in 1806. They expressly declared that their aim was only to provide for the education of such poor children as were not provided for by any religious society; for at that time the whole theory of education was that it should be religious, and almost all schools were sectarian. The

The free schools increased in number and finally grew to be called public schools.

free schools increased in number under the care of the society, and finally grew to be called public schools; and by growth and change the system was gradually transformed, until one of the cardinal points of public policy in New York, as elsewhere in the northern United States, became the establishment of free, non-sectarian public schools, supported and managed by the

State, and attended by the great mass of the children who go to school at all. The sectarian schools, all-important before the rise of the public-school system, have now been thrust into an entirely secondary position. Perhaps the best work of the public school has been in the direction of Americanizing immigrants, or rather the children of immigrants; and it would be almost impossible to overestimate the good it has accomplished in this direction.

The city began to have room for an occasional man of letters or science, in addition to the multitude of lawyers and clergymen.

Many scientific and literary societies were founded in New York early in the present century. The city began to have room for an occasional man of letters or science, in addition to the multitude of lawyers and clergymen,—the lawyer, in particular, occupying the front rank in Revolutionary and post-Revolutionary days. A queer, versatile scholar and student of science, who also dabbled in politics and philanthropy, Dr. Samuel Latham Mitchell, was one of New York's most prominent and most eccentric characters at this time. Charles Brockden Brown published one or two mystical novels which in their day had a certain vogue, even across the Atlantic, but are now only remembered as being the earliest American ventures of the kind; and in 1807 Washington Irving may be said to have first broken ground in the American field of true literature with his "Knickerbocker's History of New York."

This same year of 1807 was rendered noteworthy by the beginning of steam navigation. Robert Fulton, after many failures, at last invented a model that would work, and took his steamboat, the Clermont, on a trial trip from New York to Albany and back. Thus he began the era of travel by steam, to which, more than to any other one of the many marvellous discoveries and inventions of the age, we owe the mighty and far-reaching economic and social changes which this century has witnessed. Fulton's claim to the discovery was disputed by a score of men,—among them his fellow-citizens, John Fitch, Nicholas Roosevelt, and John Stevens, all of whom had built steamboats which had just not succeeded. But the fact remained that he was the first one to apply the principle successfully; and to him the credit belongs. Very soon there were a number of American steamboats in existence. In 1811 Nicholas Roosevelt introduced them on the Mississippi, while Stevens took his to the Delaware. During the War of 1812 Fulton planned and built at New York, under the direction of Congress, a great steam frigate, with cannon-proof sides and heavy guns; she worked well, but peace was declared just before she was ready, otherwise she would probably have anticipated the feats of the Merrimac by half a century.

It was a calamity to the city that this steam frigate was not ready earlier; for New York was blockaded closely throughout this war, which was far from popular with her merchants. Yet they ought to have seen that the war was most necessary to their commercial well-being, no less than to their honour and national self-respect; for the frigates of Britain had for a dozen years of nominal peace kept the city under a more or less severe blockade, in the exercise of the odious right of search. They kept a strict watch over all outgoing and incoming ships, hovering off the coast like hawks, and cruising in the lower bay, firing on coasters and merchantmen to bring them to.

Once they even killed one of the crew of a coaster in this manner, and the outrage went unavenged. When war at last came, many of the ardent young men of the city, who had chafed under the insults to which they had been exposed, went eagerly into the business of privateering, which combined both profit and revenge. New York sent scores of privateers to sea to prey on the enemy's commerce; and formidable craft they were, especially toward the end of the war, when the typical privateer was a large brig or schooner of wonderful speed and beauty, well armed and heavily manned. The lucky cruiser, when many prizes were taken, brought wealth to owner, captain, and crew; and some of the most desperate sea-struggles of the kind on record took place between New York privateers of this day and boat expeditions, sent to cut them out by hostile frigates or squadrons,—the most famous instance being the really remarkable fight of the brig "General Armstrong" at Fayal.

With the close of the war, the beginning of immigration from Europe on a vast scale, and the adoption of a more radically democratic State constitution, the history of old New

York may be said to have come to an end, and that of the modern city, with its totally different conditions, to have begun. The town has never, before or since, had a population so nearly homogeneous as just after this second war with Great Britain; the English blood has never been so nearly dominant as at that time, nor the English speech so nearly the sole speech in common use. The Dutch language had died out, and the Dutch themselves had become completely assimilated. With the Huguenot French this was even more completely the case.[6] German was only spoken by an insignificant and dwindling remnant. Of the Irish immigrants, most had become absorbed in the population; the remainder was too small to be of any importance. The negroes no longer formed a noteworthy element in the population, and gradual emancipation, begun in 1799, became complete by 1827. For thirty-five years after the Revolution the great immigration was from New England, and the consequent influx of nearly pure English blood was enormous. The old New Yorkers regarded this "New England

---

[6] However, one Huguenot church has always kept up its language, mainly for the use of foreigners.

invasion," as they called it, with jealous hostility; but this feeling was a mere sentiment, for the newcomers speedily became almost indistinguishable from the old residents. Even in religious matters the people were more in unison than ever before or since. The bitter jealousies and antagonisms between the different Protestant sects, so characteristic of colonial times, had greatly softened; and Roman Catholicism was not as yet of importance. There was still no widespread and grinding poverty, and there were no colossal fortunes. The conditions of civic or municipal life then were in no way akin to what they are now, and none of the tremendous problems with which we must now grapple had at that time arisen.

There was still no widespread and grinding poverty, and there were no colossal fortunes.

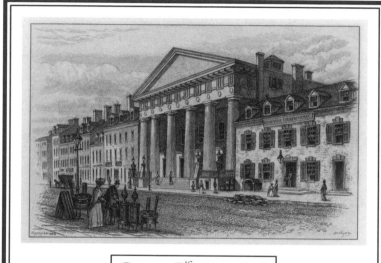

Bowery Theatre, 1826.

1821-1860
The Growth of the Commercial and Democratic City.

THE DISTINGUISHING features of the life of the city between 1820 and 1860 were its steady and rapid growth in population, the introduction of an absolutely democratic system of government, the immense immigration from abroad, completely changing the ethnic character of the population, the wonderful growth of the Roman Catholic Church, and the great material prosperity, together with the vast fortunes made by many of the business men, usually of obscure and humble ancestry.

The opening of the Erie Canal gave an extraordinary impetus to the development of the city. The canal had been planned, and reports concerning it drawn up, at different times by various New York citizens, notably by Gouverneur Morris;

but the work was actually done, in spite of violent opposition, by De Witt Clinton. Clinton was, more than any other man, responsible for the introduction of the degrading system of spoils politics into the State; most of his political work was mere faction fighting for his own advancement; and he was too jealous of all competitors, and at the same time not a great enough man, ever to become an important figure in the national arena. But he was sincerely proud of his city and State, and very much interested in all philanthropic, scientific, and industrial movements to promote their honour and material welfare. He foresaw the immense benefits that would be brought about by the canal, and the practicability of constructing it; and by indomitable resolution and effort he at last committed the State to the policy he wished. In 1817 the work was started, and in 1825 it was completed, and the canal opened.

Fulton and Morse stand as typical of the inventive, mechanical, and commercial genius of the city.

During the same period regular lines of steamboats were established on both the Hudson and the Sound; and the steamboat service soon became of great commercial importance. It was a couple of decades later before the railroads became factors in the city's development, but they soon completely distanced the steamboats, and finally even the canal itself; and as line after line multiplied, they became the great inland feeders of New York's commerce. The electric telegraph likewise was introduced before the middle of the century; and, as with the steamboat, its father, the man who first put it into practical operation, was a New Yorker, Samuel Morse,—though there were scores of men who had perceived its possibilities, and vainly striven to translate them into actual usefulness. Steam transportation and electricity have been the two prime factors in the great commercial and industrial revolutions of this century; and New York has produced the two men who deserve the most credit for their introduction. Fulton and Morse stand as typical of the inventive, mechanical, and commercial genius of the city at the mouth of the Hudson.

Few commercial capitals have ever grown with more marvellous rapidity than New York. The great merchants and men of affairs who have built up her material prosperity, have not merely enriched themselves and their city; they have also played no inconsiderable part in that rapid opening up of the American continent during the present century, which has been rendered possible by the eagerness and far-reaching business ambition of commercial adventurers, wielding the wonderful tools forged by the science of our day. The merchant, the "railroad king," the capitalist who works or gambles for colossal stakes, bending to his purpose an intellect in its way as shrewd and virile as that of any statesman or warrior,—all these, and their compeers, are and have been among the most striking and important, although far from the noblest, figures of nineteenth-century America.

Two New Yorkers of great note in this way may be instanced as representatives of their class,—John Jacob Astor and Cornelius Vanderbilt. Astor was originally a German pedler, who came to the city immediately after the close of the Revolution. He went into the retail fur-trade, and by energy, thrift, and far-sightedness, soon pushed his way up so as to be able to command a large amount of capital; and he forthwith embarked on ventures more extensive in scale. The fur-trade was then in the North almost what the trade in gold and silver had been in the South. Vast fortunes were made in it, and the career of the fur-trader was checkered by romantic successes and hazardous vicissitudes. Astor made money with great rapidity, and entered on a course of rivalry with the huge fur companies of Canada. Finally, in 1809, he organized the American Fur Company, under the auspices of the State of New York, with no less a purpose than the establishment of a settlement of trappers and fur-traders at the mouth of the Columbia. He sent his parties out both by sea and overland, established his posts, and drove a thriving trade; and doubtless he would have anticipated by a generation the permanent settlement of Oregon, if the war had not broken out, and his colony been destroyed by the British. The most substantial portion of his fortune was made out of successful ventures in New York City real estate; and at his death he was one of the five richest men in the world. His greatest service to the city was founding the Astor Library.

Vanderbilt was a Staten Island boy, whose parents were very poor, and who therefore had to work for his living at an early age. Before the War of 1812, when a lad in his teens, he had been himself sailing a sloop as a ferry-boat, between Staten Island and New York, and soon had saved enough money to start a small line of them. After the war he saw the possibilities of the steamboat, and began to run one as captain, owning a share in it as well. He shortly saved enough to become his own capitalist, and removed to New York in 1829. He organized steam lines on the Hudson and Sound, making money hand over hand; and in 1849—the period of the California gold fever—he turned his attention to ocean steamships, and for several years carried on a famous contest with the Pacific Mail Steamship Company, for the traffic across the Isthmus to California. He was drawn into antagonism with the filibuster Walker, because of his connection with the Central American States, and became one of the forces which compassed that gray-eyed adventurer's downfall. Then he took to building and managing railways, and speculating in them, and by the end of his days had amassed a colossal fortune. The history of the Wall Street speculations in which he took part, forms much the least attractive portion of the record of his life.

Astor and Vanderbilt were foremost and typical representatives of the commercial New York of their day, exactly as Hamilton and Jay were of the Revolutionary and post-Revolutionary city. Neither was of English blood; Astor was a German, and Vanderbilt a descendant of the old Dutch settlers. Both were of obscure parentage, and both hewed their way up from the ranks by sheer force of intellect and will-power. Of course neither deserves for a moment to be classed on the city's roll of honour with men like Hamilton and Jay, or like Cooper and Irving.

Before the days of steamship, railroad, and telegraph, were the days of the fast "clippers," whose white wings sped over the ocean up to the time of the Civil War. The New York clippers, like those of Baltimore, were famous for their speed, size, and beauty. Their builders exhausted every expedient to bring them to

The Wall Street speculations in which [Vanderbilt] took part, forms the least attractive portion of his life.

perfection; and for many years after steamers were built they maintained a nearly equal fight against these formidable rivals.

Crack vessels among them repeatedly made the voyage to England in a fortnight. It is a curious fact that the United States, which only rose to power at the very end of the period of sailing-vessels, and which has not been able to hold her own among those nations whose sons go down to the sea in ships, should nevertheless, during the first half of the present century, have brought the art of building, handling—and when necessary, fighting—these same old-time sailing-ships, in all their varieties of man-of-war, privateer, merchantman, and whaler, to the highest point ever attained. The frigates and privateers were perfected during the War of 1812; the merchant clippers were immensely improved after that date. The older vessels were slow, tubby craft; and they were speedily superseded by the lines of swift packet-ships,—such as the "Blackball," "Red Star," and "Swallow Tail,"—established one after the other by enterprising and venturesome New York merchants. The packet-ships sailed for European ports. Before the middle of the century, lines of clippers were established to trade, and also to carry passengers to California and the China seas. In size they sometimes went up to two thousand tons; and compared to European merchant vessels, their speed and safety were such that they commanded from shippers half as much again in payment for the freightage on cargoes of teas and other Eastern goods.

The large importers, and their captains as well, made money rapidly by these ships; yet now, from divers causes, the carrying-trade has slipped through their fingers. But the city's growth has not been checked by this loss. The commerce-bringing fleets of other nations throng its harbour, while its merchants retain their former energy, and command their former success in other lines; and the steady and rapid growth of factories of many kinds has changed the city into a great manufacturing centre. There is no danger of any loss of commercial prosperity, nor of any falling off in the amount of wealth as a whole, nor of any diminution in the ranks of the men who range from well-to-do to very rich. The danger arises from the increase of grinding poverty among vast masses of the population in certain quarters, and from the real or seeming increase in the inequality of conditions between the very rich and the very poor; in other words, as colossal fortunes grow up on the one hand, there grows up on the other a large tenement-house population, partly composed of wage-earners who never save anything, and partly of those who never earn quite enough to give their families even the necessaries of life.

A really great piece of architectural engineering was the Croton aqueduct.

Throughout this period New York's public and private buildings were increasing in size and costliness as rapidly as in numbers. It is difficult to say as much for their beauty, as a whole. Nevertheless, some of them are decidedly handsome,— notably some of the churches, such as Trinity, and above all St. Patrick's, the cornerstone of which was laid in 1858. A really great piece of architectural engineering was the Croton aqueduct which was opened for use in 1842.

The city had also done something for that higher national development, the lack of which makes material prosperity simply a source of national vulgarization. She did her share in helping forward the struggling schools of American painters and sculptors; and she did more than her share in founding American literature. Sydney Smith's famous query, propounded in 1820, was quite justified by the facts. Nobody of the present day does read any American book which was then written, with two exceptions; and the witty Dean could scarcely be expected to have any knowledge of Irving's first purely local work, while probably hardly a soul in England had so much as heard of that really wonderful volume, "The Federalist." Both of these were New York books; and New York may fairly claim to have been the birthplace of American literature. Immediately after 1820 Washington Irving and Fenimore Cooper won world-wide fame; while Bryant was chief of a group of poets which included men like Rodman Drake. For the first time we had a literature worthy of being so called, which was not saturated with the spirit of servile colonialism, the spirit of humble imitation of things European. Our political life became full and healthy only after we had achieved political independence; and it is quite as true that we never have done, and never shall do, anything really worth doing, whether in literature or art, except when working distinctively as Americans.

We are not yet free from the spirit of colonialism in art and letters; but the case was, and is, much worse with our purely social life,—or at least with that portion of it which ought to be, and asserts itself to be, but emphatically is not, our best social life. In the "Potiphar Papers," Mr. Curtis, a New Yorker of whom all New Yorkers can be proud, has left a description which can hardly be called a caricature of fashionable New York society as it was in the decade before the war. It is not an attractive picture. The city then contained nearly three quarters of a million inhabitants, and the conditions of life were much as they are to-day. The era of railroads and steamships was well under way; all the political and social problems and evils which now exist, existed then, often in aggravated form. The mere commercial classes were absorbed in making money,—a pursuit which of course becomes essentially ignoble when followed as an end and not as a means. It had become very easy to travel in Europe, and immense shoals of American tourists went thither every season, deriving but doubtful benefit from their tour. New York possessed a large wealthy class which did not quite know how to get most pleasure from its money, and which had not been trained, as all good citizens of the republic should be trained, to realize that in America every man of means and leisure must do some kind of work, whether in politics, in literature, in science, or in what, for lack of a better word, may be called philanthropy, if he wishes really to enjoy life, and to avoid being despised as a drone in the community. Moreover, they failed to grasp the infinite possibilities of enjoyment, of interest, and of usefulness, which American life offers to every man, rich or poor, if he have only heart and head. With

New York possessed a large wealthy class which did not quite know how to get most pleasure from its money.

singular poverty of imagination they proceeded on the assumption that to enjoy their wealth they must slavishly imitate the superficial features, and the defects rather than the merits, of the life of the wealthy classes of Europe, instead of borrowing only its best traits, and adapting even these to their own surroundings. They put wealth above everything else, and therefore hopelessly vulgarized their lives. The shoddy splendours of the second French Empire naturally appealed to them, and so far as might be they imitated its ways. Dress, manners, amusements,—all were copied from Paris; and when they went to Europe, it was in Paris that they spent most of their time. To persons of intelligence and force their lives seemed equally dull at home and abroad. They took little interest in literature or politics; they did not care to explore and hunt and travel in their own country; they did not have the taste for athletic sport which is so often the one redeeming feature of the gilded youth of to-day, and which, if not very much when taken purely by itself, is at least something. Fashionable society was composed of two classes. There were, first, the people of good family,—those whose forefathers at some time had played their parts manfully in the world, and who claimed some shadowy superiority on the strength of this memory of the past, unbacked by any proof of merit in the present. Secondly, there were those who had just made money,—the father having usually merely the money-getting faculty, the presence of which does not necessarily imply the existence of any other worthy quality whatever, the rest of the family possessing only the absorbing desire to spend what the father had earned. In the summer they all went to Saratoga or to Europe; in winter they came back to New York. Fifth Avenue was becoming the fashionable street, and on it they built their brownstone-front houses, all alike outside, and all furnished in the same style within,—heavy furniture, gilding, mirrors, glittering chandeliers. If a man was very rich he had a few feet more frontage, and more gilding, more mirrors, and more chandeliers. There was one incessant round of gaiety, but it possessed no variety whatever, and little interest.

Of course there were plenty of exceptions to all these rules. There were many charming houses, there was much pleasant social life, just as there were plenty of honest politicians; and there were multitudes of men and women well fitted to perform the grave duties and enjoy the great rewards of American life. But taken as a whole, the fashionable and political life of New York in the decade before the Civil War offers an instructive rather than an attractive spectacle.

Wall Street, 1825.

1860-1890
Recent History.

IN 1860 New York had over eight hundred thousand inhabitants. During the thirty years that have since passed, its population has nearly doubled. If the city limits were enlarged, like those of London and Chicago, so as to take in the suburbs, the population would amount to some three millions. Recently there has been a great territorial expansion northward, beyond the Haarlem, by the admission of what is known as the Annexed District. The growth of wealth has fully kept pace with the growth of population. The city is one of the two or three greatest commercial and manufacturing centres of the world.

The ten years between 1860 and 1870 form the worst decade in the city's political annals, although the sombre picture is relieved by touches of splendid heroism, martial prowess, and civic devotion. At the outbreak of the Civil War the city was—as it has since continued to be—the stronghold of the Democratic party in the North; and unfortunately, during the Rebellion, while the Democratic party contained many of the loyal, it also contained all of the disloyal, elements. A Democratic victory at the polls, hardly, if at all, less than a Confederate victory in the field, meant a Union defeat. A very large and possibly a controlling element in the city Democracy was at heart strongly disunion in sentiment, and showed the feeling whenever it dared.

At the outset of the Civil War there was even an effort made to force the city into active rebellion. The small local Democratic leaders, of the type of Isaiah Rynders, the brutal and turbulent ruffians who led the mob and controlled the politics of the lower wards, openly and defiantly threatened to make common cause with the South, and to forbid the passage of Union troops through the city. The mayor, Fernando Wood, in January, 1861, proclaimed disunion to be "a fixed fact" in a message to the Common Council, and proposed that New York should herself secede and become a free city, with but a nominal duty upon imports. The independent commonwealth was to be named "Tri-Insula," as being composed of three islands,—Long, Staten, and Manhattan. The Common Council, a corrupt body as disloyal as Wood himself, received the message enthusiastically, and had it printed and circulated wholesale.

The mayor, in January, 1861, proposed that New York should herself secede and be named "Tri-Insula."

But when Sumter was fired on the whole current changed like magic. There were many more good men than bad in New York; but they had been supine, or selfish, or indifferent, or undecided, and so the bad had had it all their own way. The thunder of Sumter's guns waked the heart of the people to passionate loyalty. The bulk of the Democrats joined with the Republicans to show by word and act their fervent and patriotic devotion to the Union. Huge mass-meetings were held, and regiment after regiment was organized and sent to the front. Shifty Fernando Wood, true to his nature, went with the stream, and was loudest in proclaiming his horror of rebellion. The city, through all her best and bravest men, pledged her faithful and steadfast support to the government at Washington. The Seventh Regiment of the New York National Guards, by all odds the best regiment in the United States Militia, was the first in the whole country to go to the front and reach Washington, securing it against any sudden surprise.

The Union men of New York kept their pledge of loyalty in spirit and letter. Taking advantage of the intensity of the loyal excitement, they even elected a Republican mayor. The New Yorkers of means were those whose part was greatest in

The Seventh Regiment of the New York National Guards was the first to go to the front.

sustaining the nation's credit, while almost every high-spirited young man in the city went into the army. The city, from the beginning to the end of the war, sent her sons to the front by scores of thousands. Her troops alone would have formed a large army; and on a hundred battle-fields, and throughout the harder trials of the long, dreary campaigns, they bore themselves with high courage and stern, unyielding resolution. Those who by a hard lot were forced to stay at home busied themselves in caring for the men at the front, or for their widows and orphans; and the Sanitary Commission, the Allotment Commission, and other kindred organizations which did incalculable good, originated in New York.

This was also the era of gigantic stock-swindling. The enormously rich stock-speculators of Wall Street in their wars with one another and against the general public, found ready tools and allies to be hired for money in the State and city politicians, and in judges who were acceptable alike to speculators, politicians, and mob. There were continual contests for the control of railway systems, and "operations" in stocks which barely missed being criminal, and which branded those who took part in them as infamous in the sight of all honest men; and the courts and legislative bodies became parties to the iniquity of men composing that most dangerous of all classes, the wealthy criminal class.

Matters reached their climax in the feats of the "Tweed Ring." William M. Tweed was the master spirit among the politicians of his own party, and also secured a hold on a number of the local Republican leaders of the baser sort.

He was a coarse, jovial, able man, utterly without scruple of any kind; and he organized all of his political allies and adherents into a gigantic "ring" to plunder the city. Incredible sums of money were stolen, especially in the construction of the new Court House. When the frauds were discovered, Tweed, secure in his power, asked in words that have become proverbial, "What are you going to do about it?" But the end came in 1871. Then the decent citizens, irrespective of party, banded together, urged on by the newspapers, especially the *Times* and *Harper's Weekly*,—for the city press deserves the chief credit for the defeat of Tweed. At the fall elections the ring candidates were overwhelmingly defeated; and the chief malefactors were afterward prosecuted, and many of them imprisoned, Tweed himself dying in a felon's cell. The offending judges were impeached, or resigned in time to escape impeachment.

The character of the immigration to the city is changing. The Irish, who in 1860 formed three fifths of the foreign-born population, have come in steadily lessening numbers, until the Germans stand well at the head; while increasing multitudes of Italians, Poles, Bohemians, Russian Jews, and Hungarians—

both Sclaves and Magyars—continually arrive. The English and
Scandinavian elements among the immigrants have likewise
increased. At the present time four fifths of New York's
population are of foreign birth or parentage; and among them
there has been as yet but little race intermixture, though the
rising generation is as a whole well on the way to complete
Americanization. Certainly hardly a tenth of the people are of
old Revolutionary American stock. The Catholic Church has
continued to grow at a rate faster than the general rate of
increase. The Episcopalian and Lutheran are the only
Protestant Churches whereof the growth has kept pace with
that of the population.

The material prosperity of the city has increased steadily.
There has been a marked improvement in architecture; and
one really great engineering work, the bridge across the East
River, was completed in 1883. The stately and beautiful
Riverside Drive, skirting the Hudson, along the hills which
front the river, from the middle of the island northward, is well
worth mention. It is one of the most striking roads or streets of
which any city can boast, and the handsome houses that are

springing up along it bid fair to make the neighbourhood the most attractive portion of New York. Another attractive feature of the city is Central Park, while many other parks are being planned and laid out beyond where the town has as yet been built up. There are large numbers of handsome social clubs, such as the Knickerbocker, Union, and University, and many others of a politico-social character,—the most noted of them, alike for its architecture, political influence, and its important past history, being the Union League Club.

There are many public buildings which are extremely interesting as showing the growth of a proper civic spirit, and of a desire for a life with higher possibilities than money-making. There has been an enormous increase in the number of hospitals, many of them admirably equipped and managed; and the numerous News-boys' Lodging Houses, Night Schools, Working-Girls' Clubs and the like, bear witness to the fact that many New Yorkers who have at their disposal time or money are alive to their responsibilities, and are actively striving to help their less fortunate fellows to help themselves. The Cooper Union building, a gift to the city for the use of all its citizens, in the widest sense, keeps alive the memory of old Peter Cooper, a man whose broad generosity and simple kindliness of character, while not rendering him fit for the public life into which he at times sought entrance, yet inspired in New Yorkers of every class a genuine regard such as they felt for no other philanthropist. Indeed, uncharitableness and lack of generosity have never been New York failings; the citizens are keenly sensible to any real, tangible distress or need. A blizzard in Dakota, an earthquake in South Carolina, a flood in Pennsylvania,—after any such catastrophe hundreds of thousands of dollars are raised in New York at a day's notice, for the relief of the

There are many public buildings which are extremely interesting as showing the growth of a proper civic spirit.

sufferers; while, on the other hand, it is a difficult matter to raise money for a monument or a work of art.

It is necessary both to appeal to the practical business sense of the citizens and to stir the real earnestness and love of country which lie underneath the somewhat coarse-grained and not always attractive surface of the community, in order to make it show its real strength. Thus, there is no doubt that in case of any important foreign war or domestic disturbance New York would back up the general government with men and money to a practically unlimited extent. For all its motley population, there is a most wholesome underlying spirit of patriotism in the city, if it can only be roused. Few will question this who saw the great processions on land and water, and the other ceremonies attendant upon the celebration of the one

> *For all its motley population, there is a most wholesome underlying spirit of patriotism in the city, if it can only be roused.*

hundredth anniversary of the adoption of the Federal Constitution. The vast crowds which thronged the streets were good-humoured and orderly to a degree, and were evidently interested in much more than the mere spectacular part of the celebration. They showed by every action their feeling that it was indeed peculiarly their celebration; for it commemorated the hundred years' duration of a government which, with many shortcomings, had nevertheless secured order and enforced law, and yet was emphatically a government of the people, giving to the workingman a chance which he has never had elsewhere. In all the poorer quarters of the city, where the population was overwhelmingly of foreign birth or origin, the national flag, the stars and stripes, hung from every window, and the picture of Washington was displayed wherever there was room. Flag and portrait alike were tokens that those who had come to our shores already felt due reverence and love for the grand memory of the man who, more than any other, laid the foundation of our government; and that they already challenged as their own American nationality and American life, glorying in the Nation's past and confident in its future.

In science and art, in musical and literary development, much remains to be wished for; yet something has already been done. The building of the Metropolitan Museum of Art, of the American Museum of Natural History, of the Metropolitan Opera House, the gradual change of Columbia College into a University,—all show a development which tends to make the city more and more attractive to people of culture; and the growth of literary and dramatic clubs, such as the Century and the Players, is scarcely less significant. The illustrated monthly magazines—the *Century, Scribner's,* and *Harper's*—occupy an entirely original position of a very high order in periodical literature. The greatest piece of literary work which has been done in America, or indeed anywhere, of recent years, was done by a citizen of New York,—not a professed man of letters, but a great General, an Ex-President of the United States, writing his memoirs on his death-bed, to save his family from want. General Grant's book has had an extraordinary sale among the people at large, though even yet hardly appreciated at its proper worth by the critics; and it is scarcely too high praise to say that, both because of the intrinsic worth of the matter, and because of its strength and simplicity as a piece of literary work, it almost deserves to rank with the speeches and writings of Abraham Lincoln.

The fact that General Grant toward the end of his life made New York his abode,—as General Sherman has since done,—illustrates what is now a well-marked tendency of prominent men throughout the country to come to this city to live. There is no such leaning toward centralization, socially or politically, in the United States as in most European countries, and no one of our cities will ever assume toward the others a position similar to that held in their own countries by London, Paris, Vienna, or Berlin. There are in the United States ten or a dozen cities each of which stands as the social and commercial, though rarely as the political, capital of a district as large as an average European kingdom. No one of them occupies a merely provincial position as compared with any other; while the political capital of the country, the beautiful city of Washington, stands apart with a most attractive and unique life of its own. There is thus no chance for New York to take an unquestioned leadership in all respects. Nevertheless, its life is so intense and so varied, and so full of manifold possibilities, that it has a special and peculiar fascination for ambitious and high-spirited men of every kind, whether they wish to enjoy the fruits of past toil, or whether they have yet their fortunes to make, and feel confident that they can swim in troubled waters,—for weaklings have small chance of forging to the front against the turbulent tide of our city life.

The truth is that every man worth his salt has open to him in New York a career of boundless usefulness and interest.

As for the upper social world, the fashionable world, it is much as it was when portrayed in the "Potiphar Papers," save that modern society has shifted the shrine at which it pays comical but sincere homage from Paris to London. Perhaps it is rather better, for it is less provincial and a trifle more American. But a would-be upper class based mainly on wealth, in which it is the exception and not the rule for a man to be of any real account in the national life, whether as a politician, a literary man, or otherwise, is of necessity radically defective and of little moment.

Its life is so intense and so varied, and so full of manifold possibilities, that it has a special and peculiar fascination.

Grim dangers confront us in the future, yet there is more ground to believe that we shall succeed than that we shall fail in overcoming them. Taking into account the enormous mass of immigrants, utterly unused to self-government of any kind, who have been thrust into our midst, and are even yet not assimilated, the wonder is not that universal suffrage has worked so badly, but that it has worked so well. We are better, not worse off, than we were a generation ago. There is much gross civic corruption and commercial and social selfishness and immorality, upon which we are in honour bound to wage active and relentless war. But honesty and moral cleanliness are the rule; and under the laws order is well preserved, and all men are kept secure in the possession of life, liberty, and property. The sons and grandsons of the immigrants of fifty years back have as a whole become good Americans, and have prospered wonderfully, both as regards their moral and material well-being. There is no reason to suppose that the condition of the working classes as a whole has grown worse, though there are enormous bodies of them whose condition is certainly very bad. There are grave social dangers and evils to meet, but there are plenty of earnest men and women who devote their minds and energies to meeting them. With many very serious shortcomings and defects, the average New Yorker yet possesses courage, energy, business capacity, much generosity of a practical sort, and shrewd, humorous common-sense. The greedy tyranny of the unscrupulous rich and the anarchic violence of the vicious and ignorant poor are ever threatening dangers; but though there is every reason why we should realize the gravity of the perils ahead of us, there is none why we should not face them with confident and resolute hope, if only each of us, according to the measure of his capacity, will with manly honesty and good faith do his full share of the all-important duties incident to American citizenship.

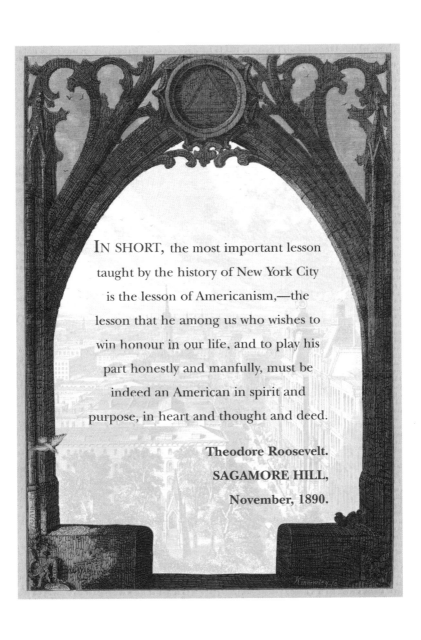

IN SHORT, the most important lesson
taught by the history of New York City
is the lesson of Americanism,—the
lesson that he among us who wishes to
win honour in our life, and to play his
part honestly and manfully, must be
indeed an American in spirit and
purpose, in heart and thought and deed.

Theodore Roosevelt.
SAGAMORE HILL,
November, 1890.

Acknowledgments

Kathleen Dalton, the author of *Theodore Roosevelt: A Strenuous Life*, was the inspiration for this book. After hearing her speak so warmly of TR, we were spurred to uncover a work that captured some of the same heroic and human qualities of this larger-than-life leader.

Our thanks also to the New York Public Library, in particular Thomas Lisanti, for making a treasure trove of historical images so accessible.

The image on the cover is from an 1872 print by Augustus F. Kinnersley titled "A glimpse of New York from Trinity Church steeple." An 1898 edition of *Munsey's Magazine* is the source for the print titled "New Amsterdam, now called New York," dated 1667 and featured in the chapter covering 1664 to 1674.

All other images are from *Old New York*, by the artist and engraver Samuel Hollyer (1826-1919).

Uncommon Books
for Serious Readers

Feeding the Mind
by Lewis Carroll

A Fortnight in the Wilderness
by Alexis de Tocqueville

Painting as a Pastime
by Winston S. Churchill

Rare Words
and ways to master
their meanings
by Jan Leighton
and Hallie Leighton

Samuel Johnson's Dictionary
Selections from the 1755 work
that defined the English language
Edited by Jack Lynch

Samuel Johnson's Insults
Edited by Jack Lynch

The Silverado Squatters
Six selected chapters
by Robert Louis Stevenson

**Sir Winston Churchill's Life
Through His Paintings**
by David Coombs
with Minnie Churchill
Foreword by Mary Soames

Words That Make a Difference
and how to use them
in a masterly way
by Robert Greenman

Levenger Press is the publishing arm of

LEVENGER®
TOOLS FOR SERIOUS READERS

www.Levenger.com   **800-544-0880**